AF574227

RETRIEVED

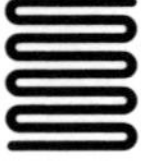

RETRIEVED

Charlotte Dumas

THE ICE PLANT • LOS ANGELES • 2011

The dogs appear in the chronological order that they were portrayed.

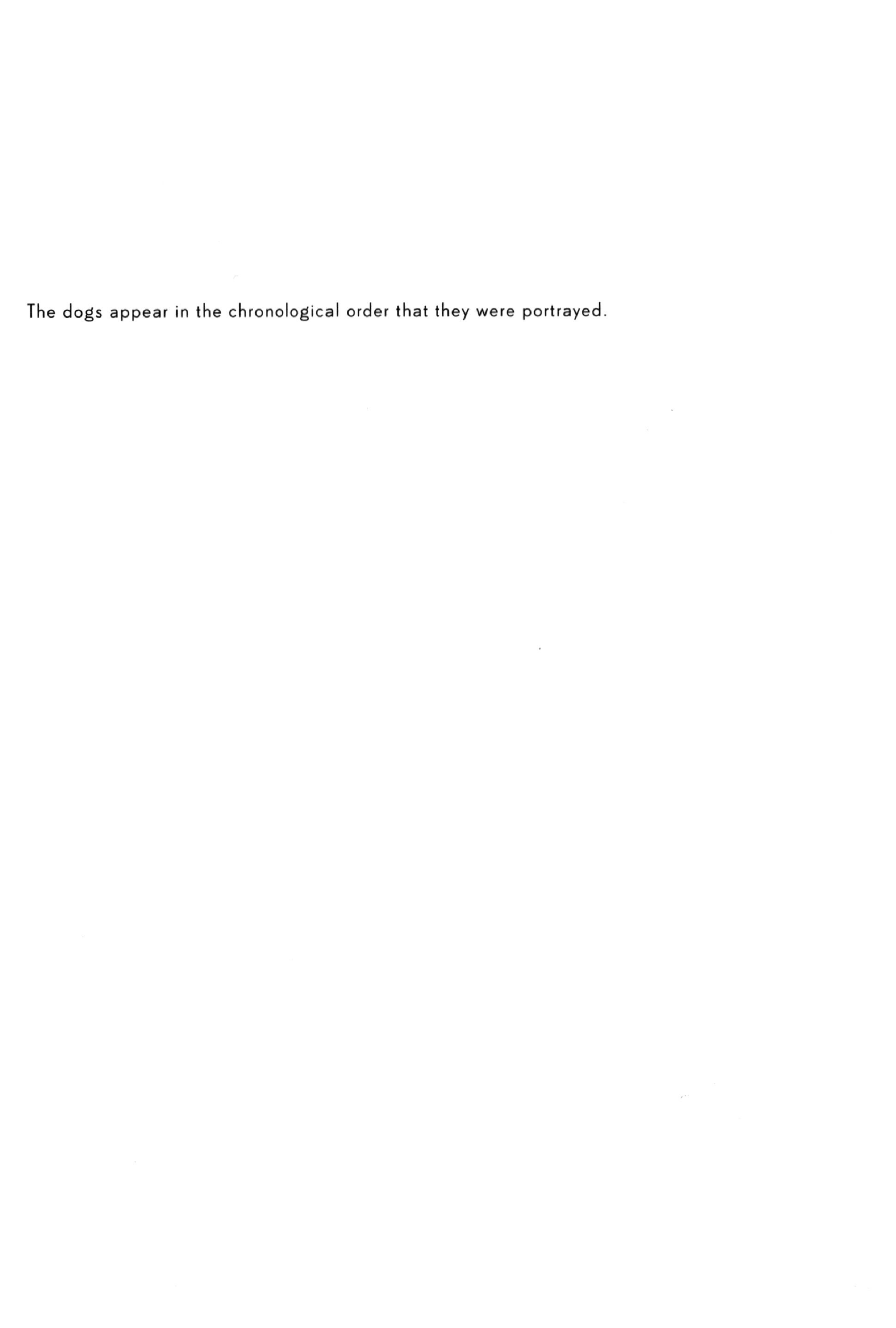

1 **MOXIE** Winthrop MA

2 **TARA** Ipswich MA

3 **SCOUT** McCordsville IN

4 **KAISER** Indianapolis IN

5 **GABRIEL** Rhoadesville VA

6 **RED** Annapolis MD

7 **GUINNESS** Highland CA

8 **DUKE** Thousand Oaks CA

9 **ABIGAIL** Ojai CA

10 **ORION** Vacaville CA

11 **TUFF** Ashland MO

12 **BAILEY** Franklin TN

13 **BRETAGNE** Cypress TX

14 **MERLYN** Otis CO

15 **HOKE** Denver CO

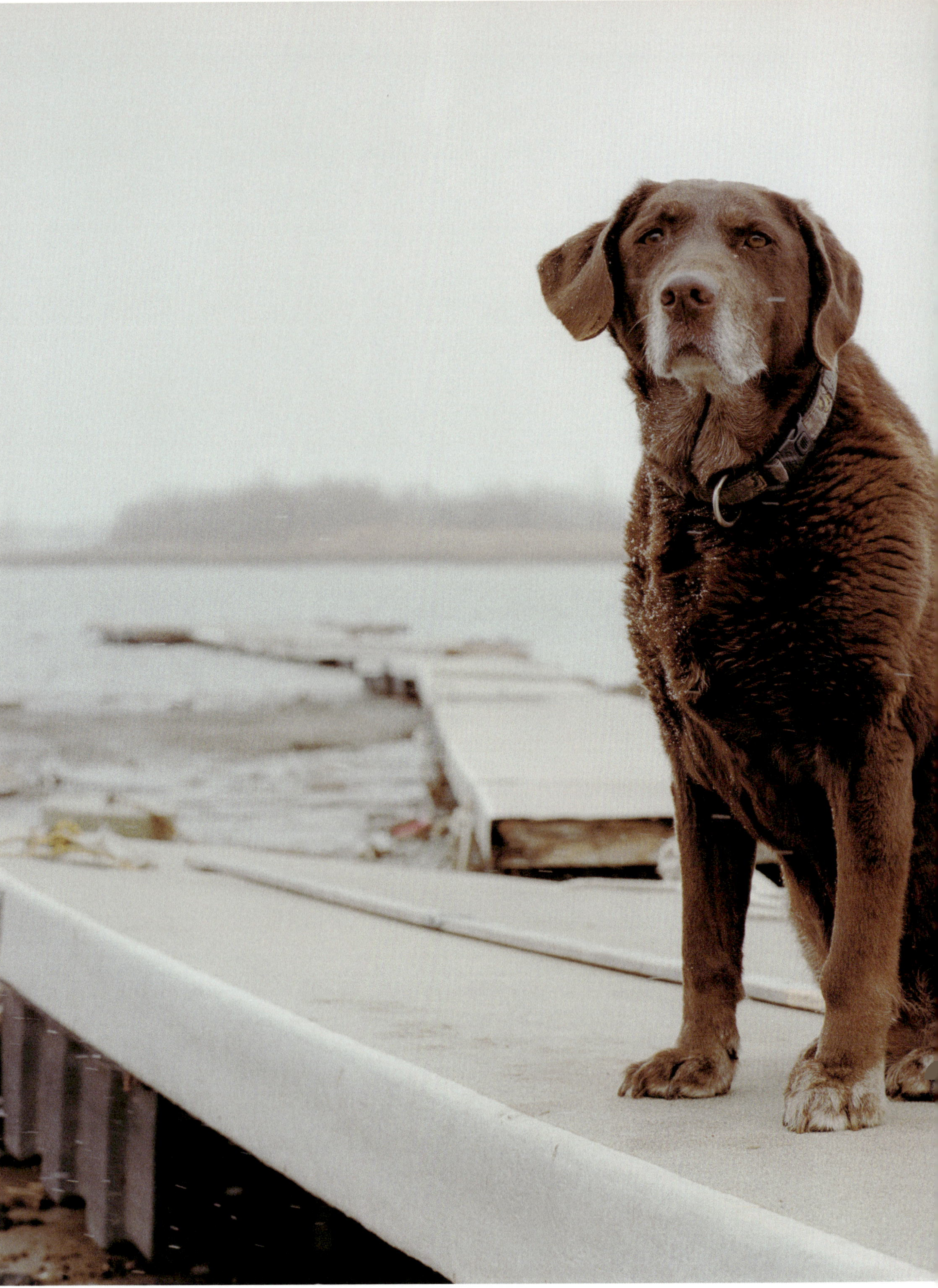

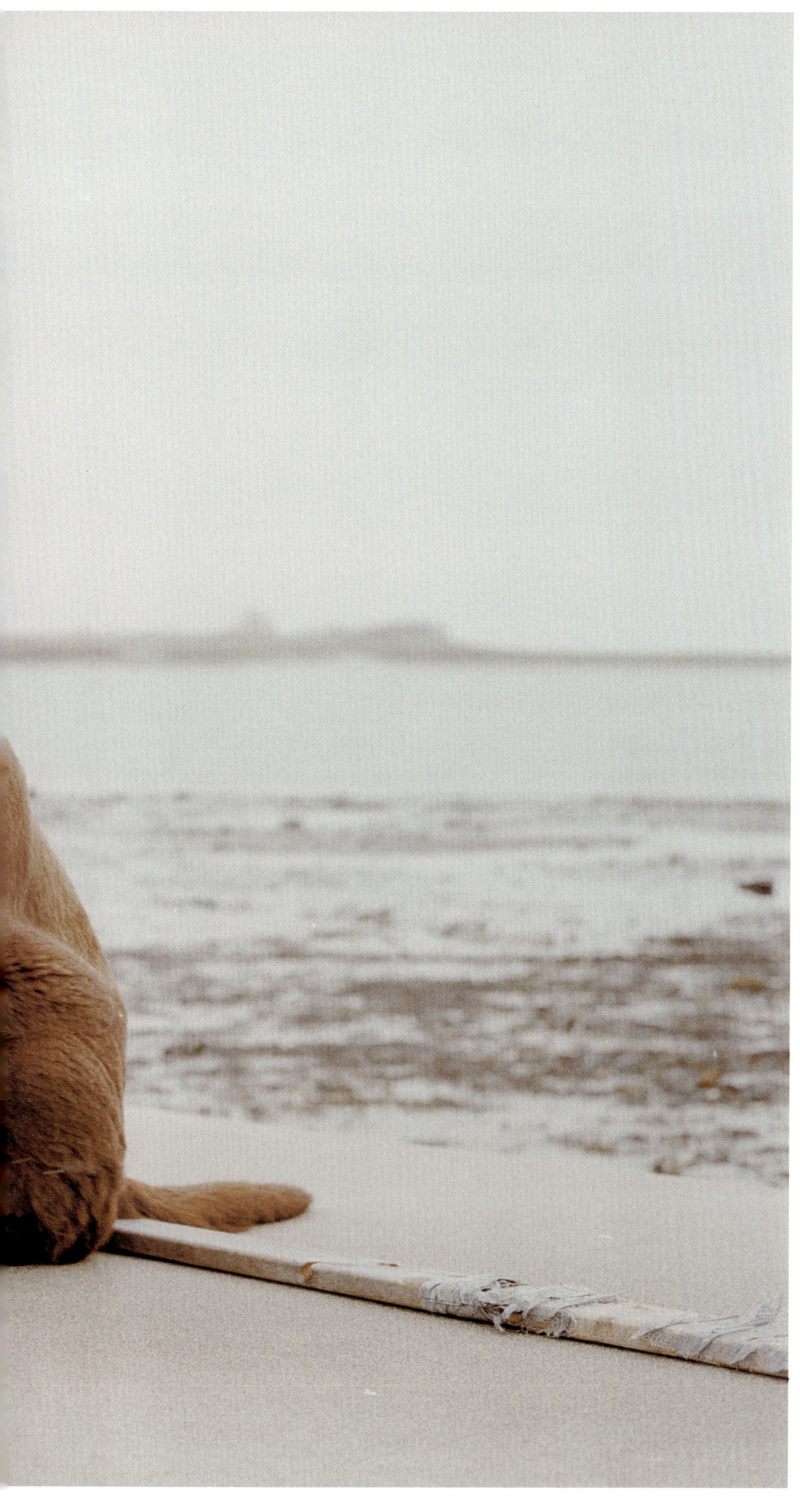

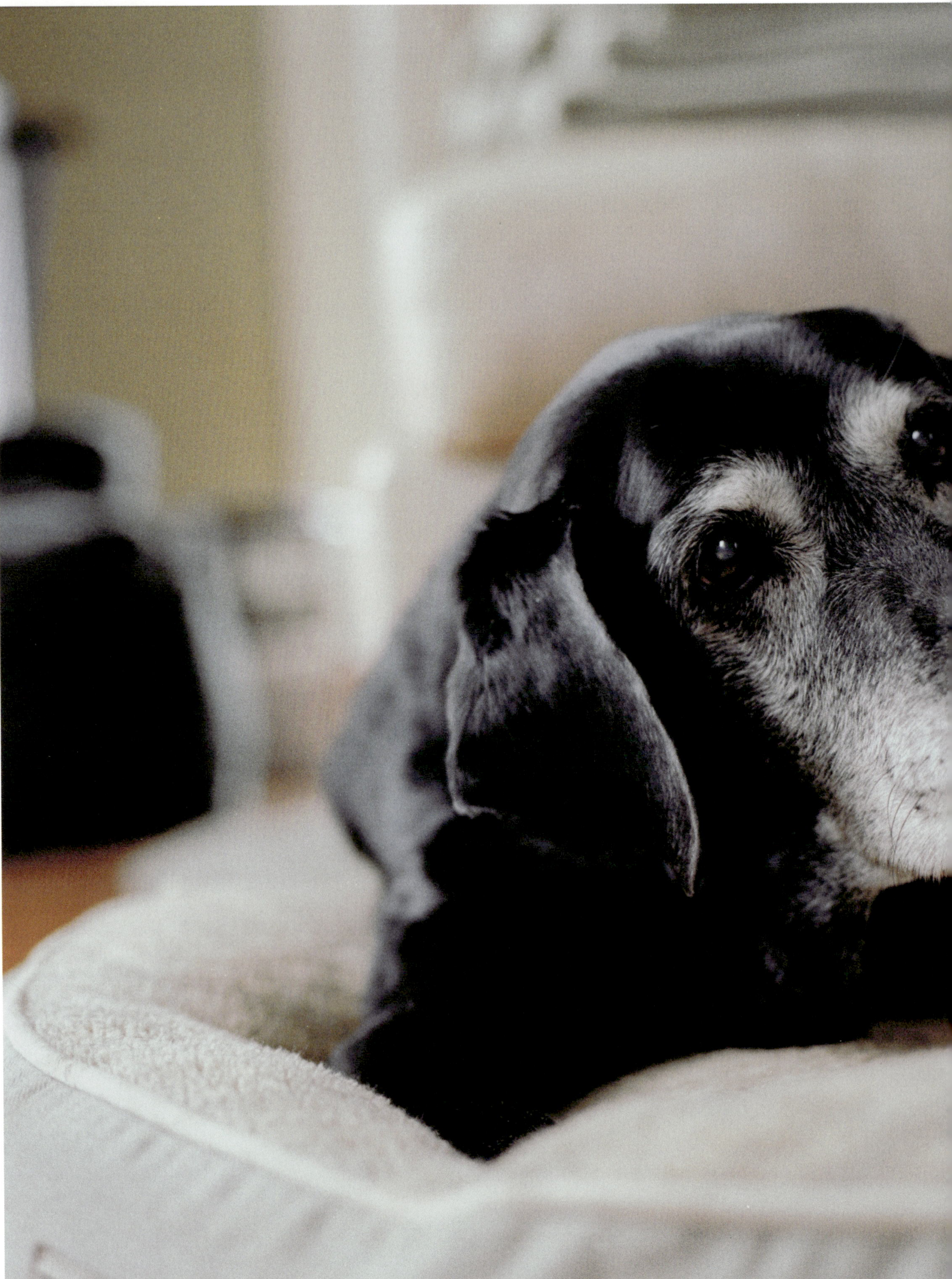

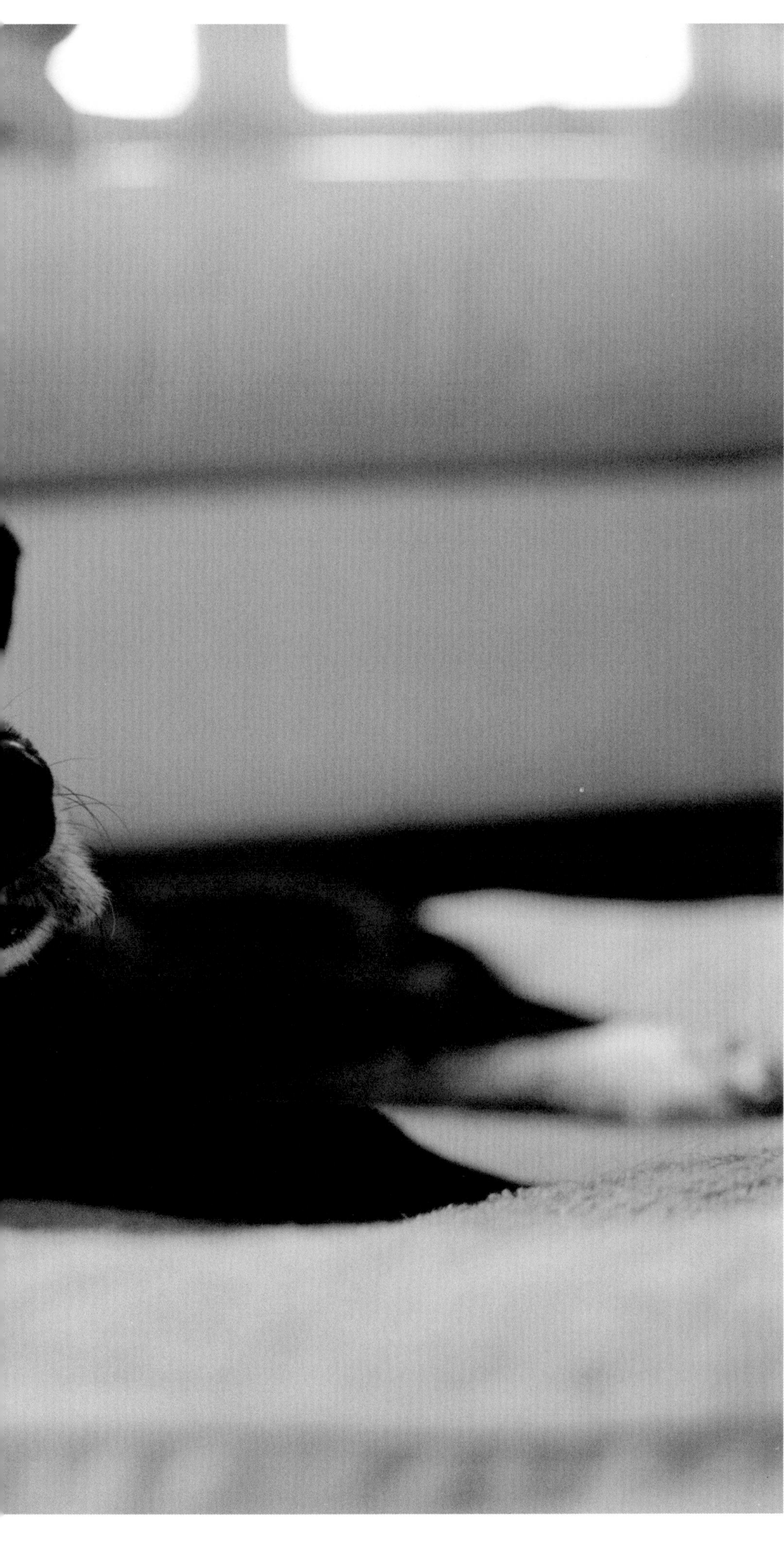

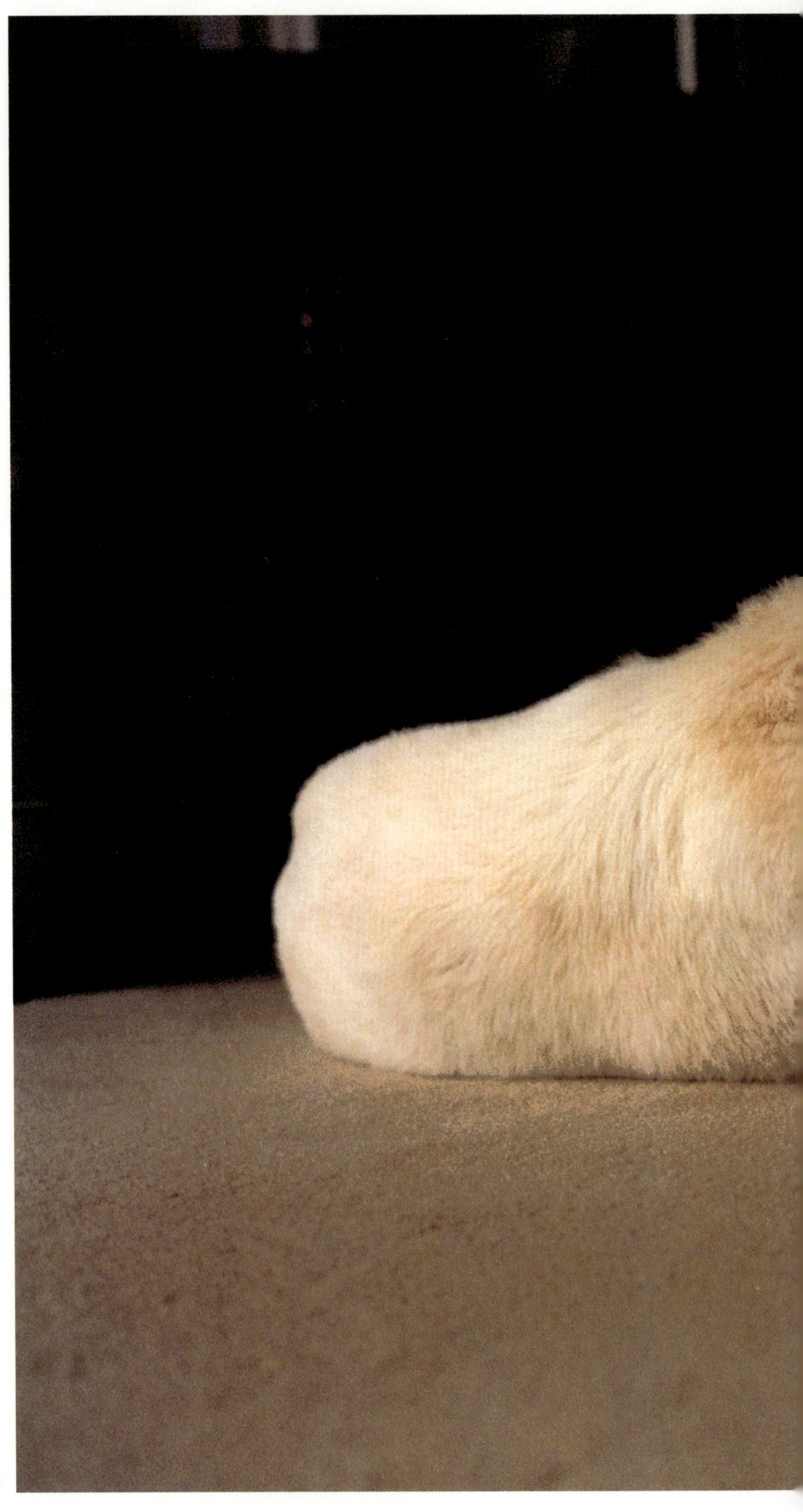

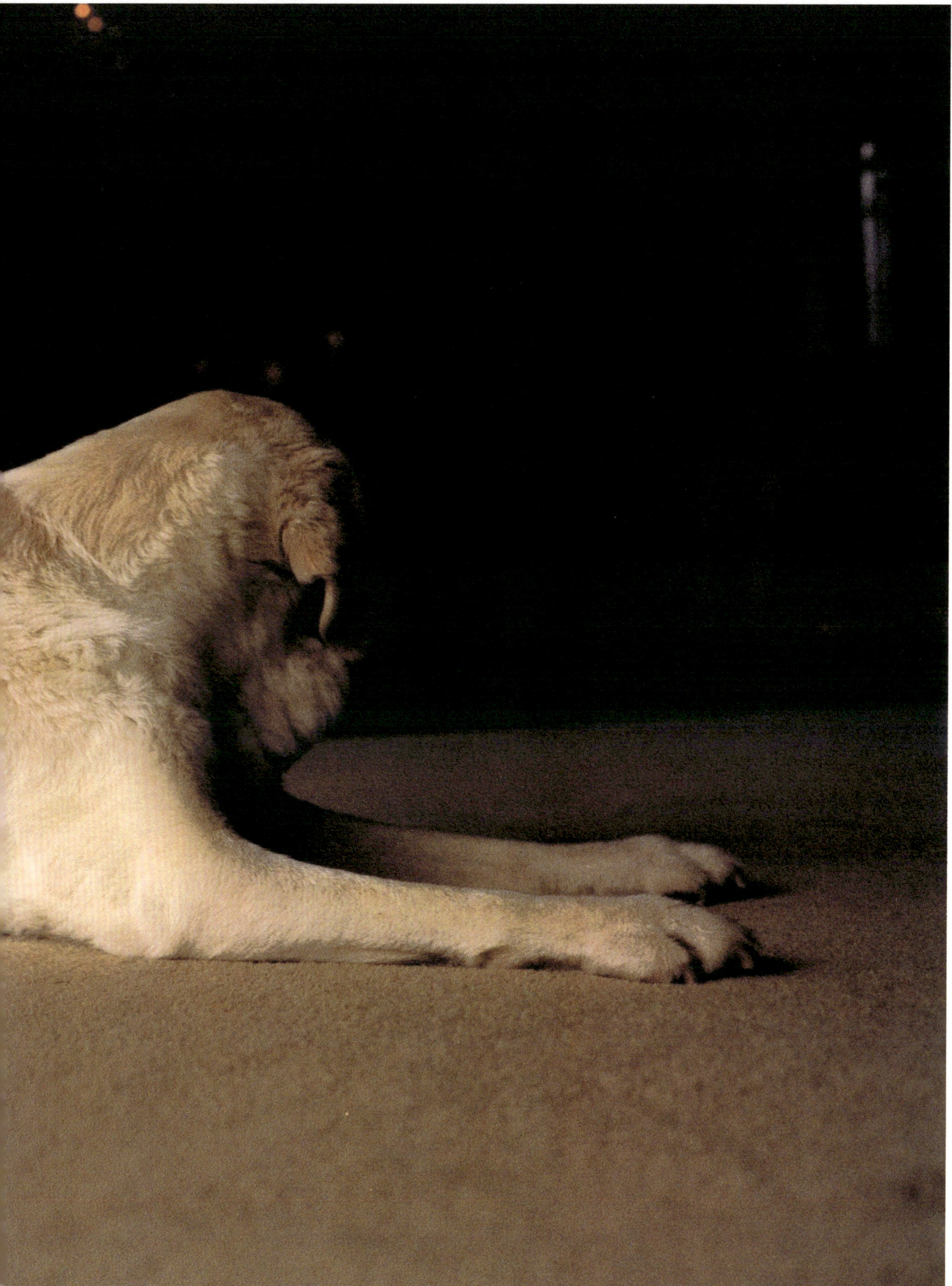

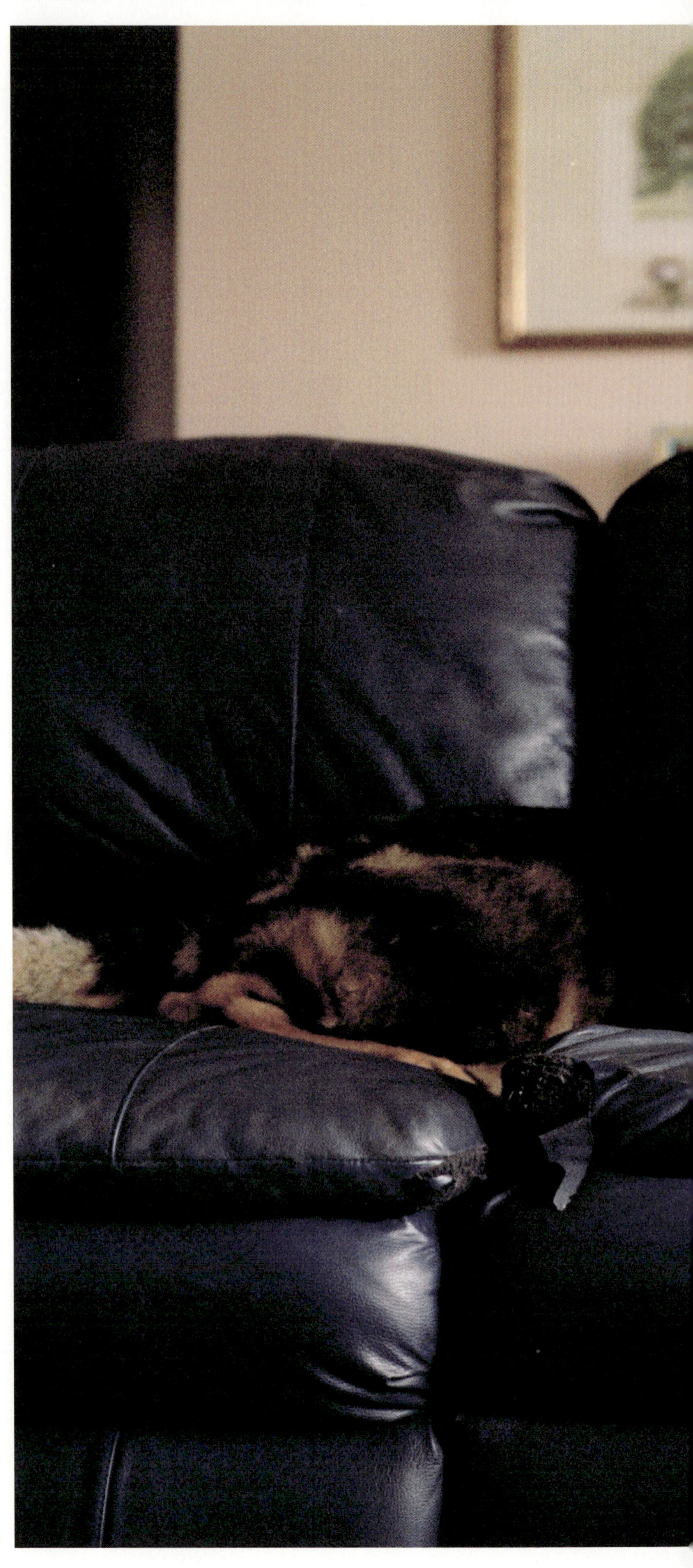

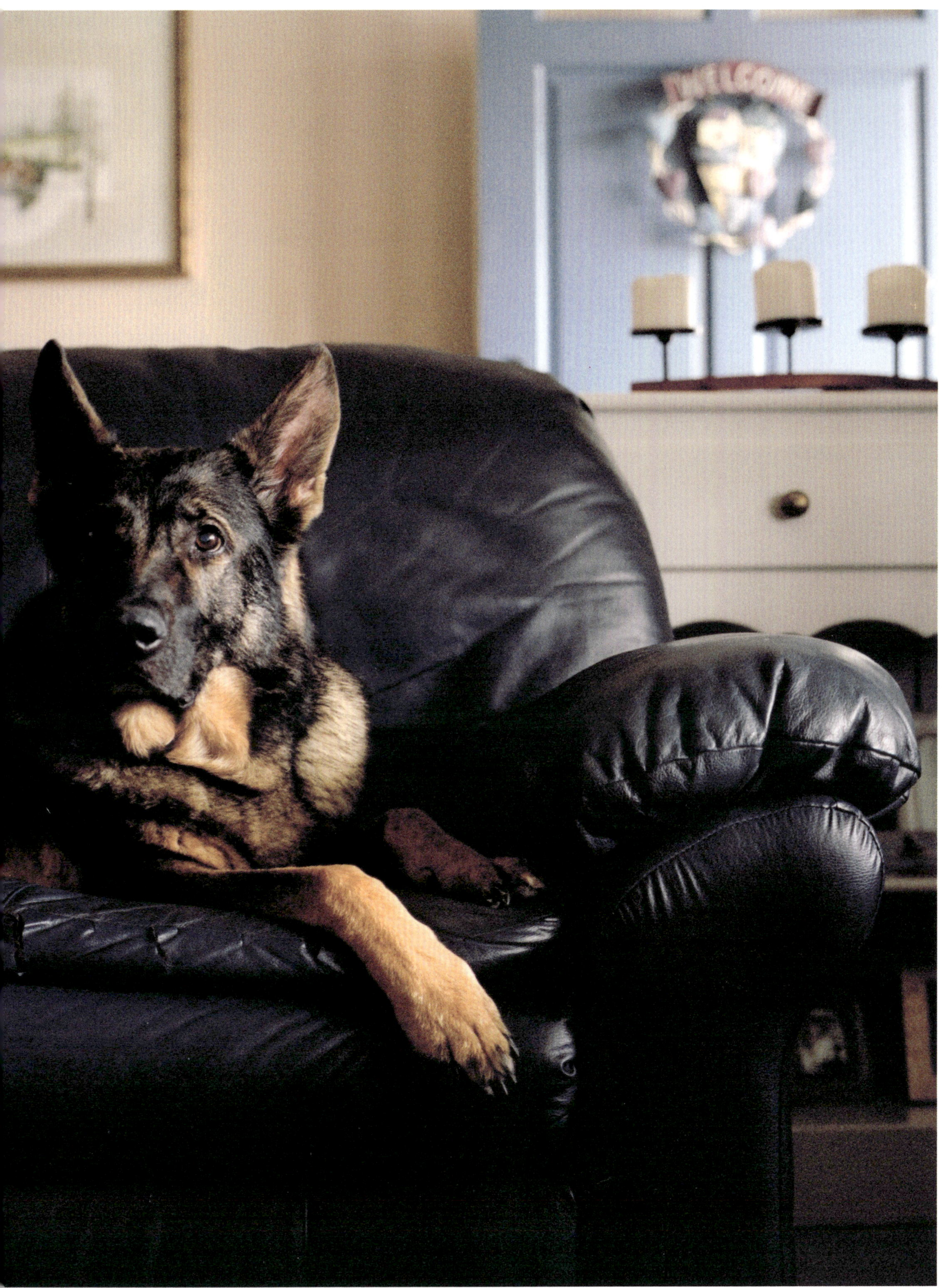

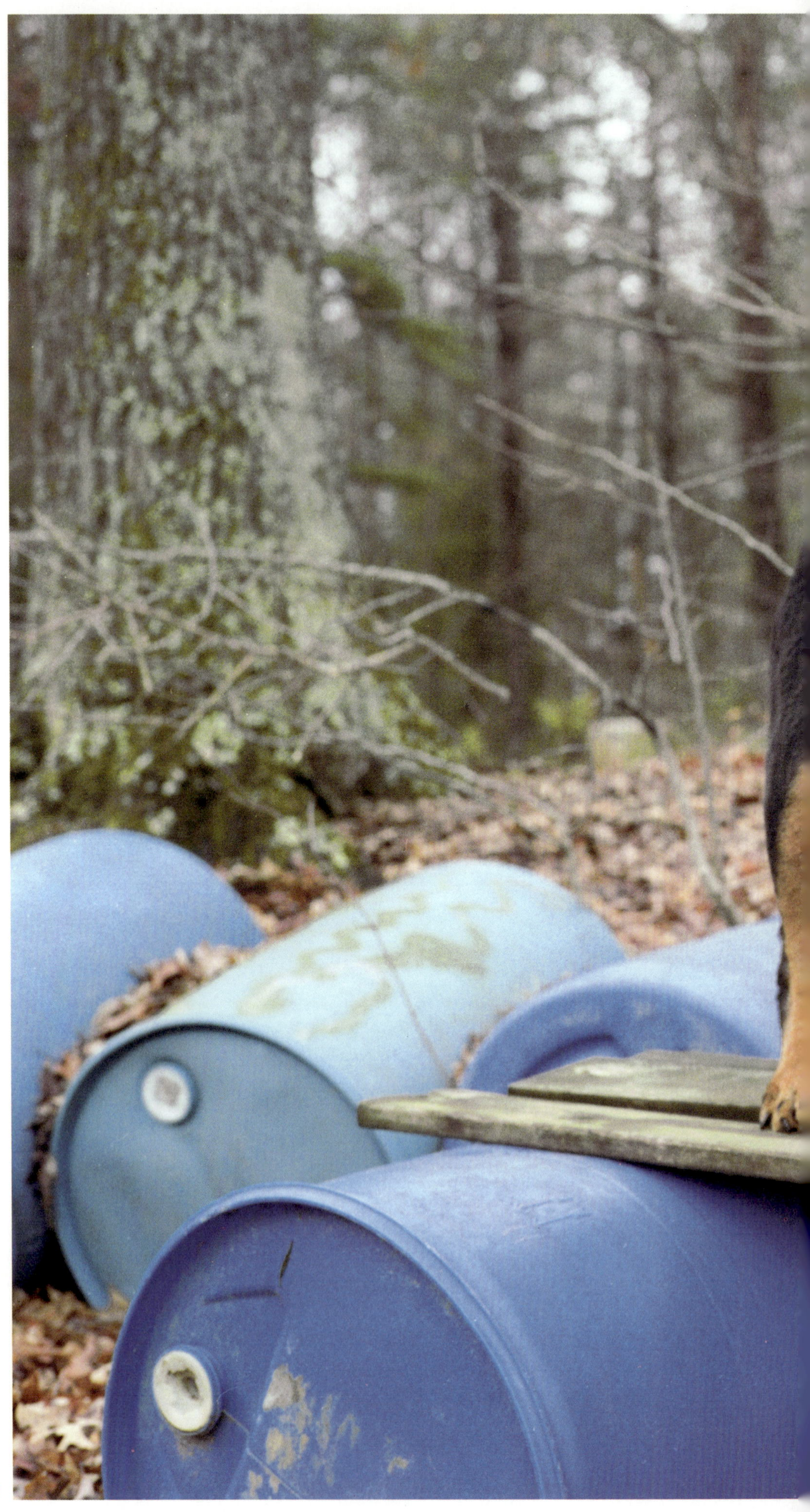

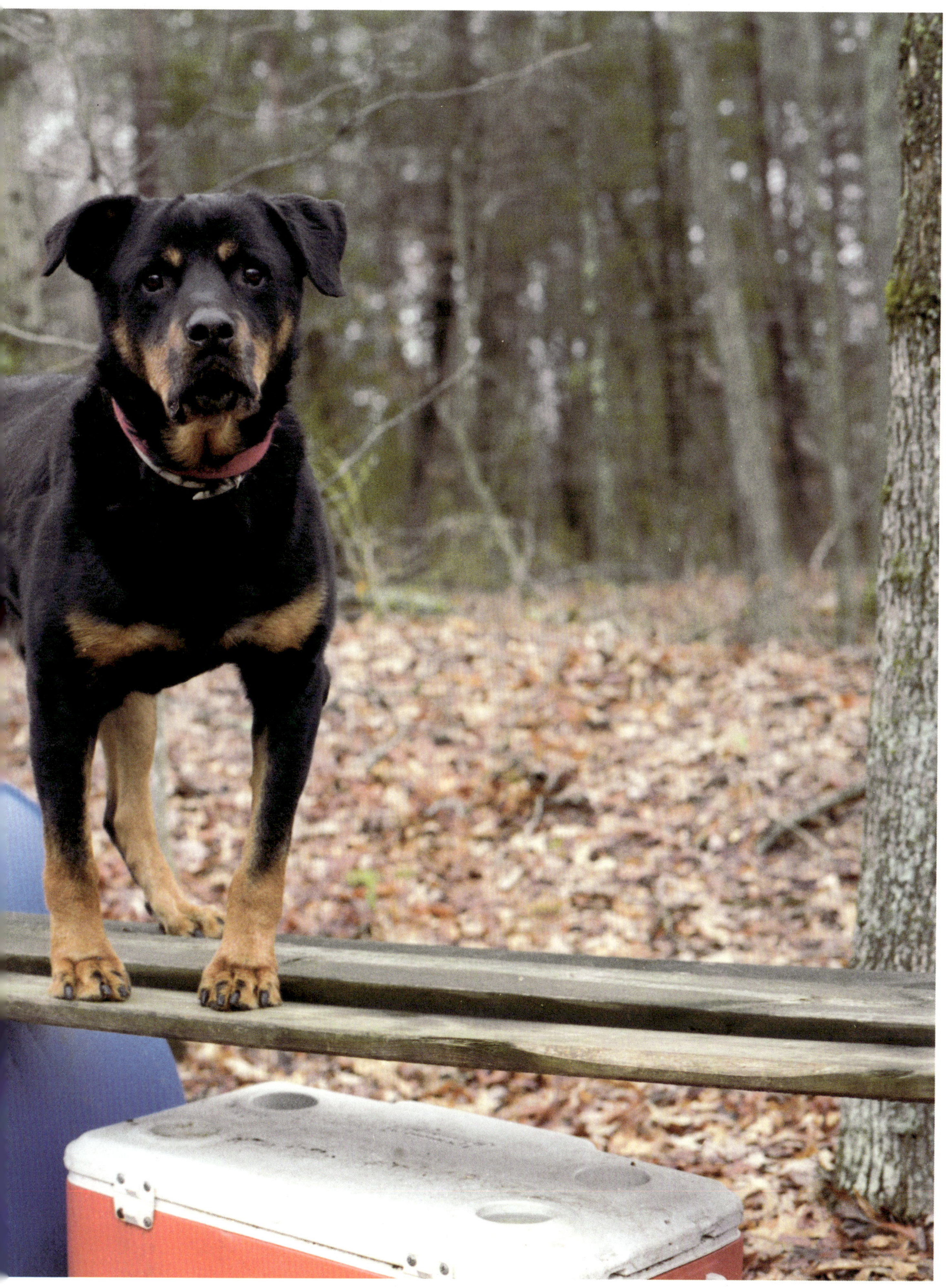

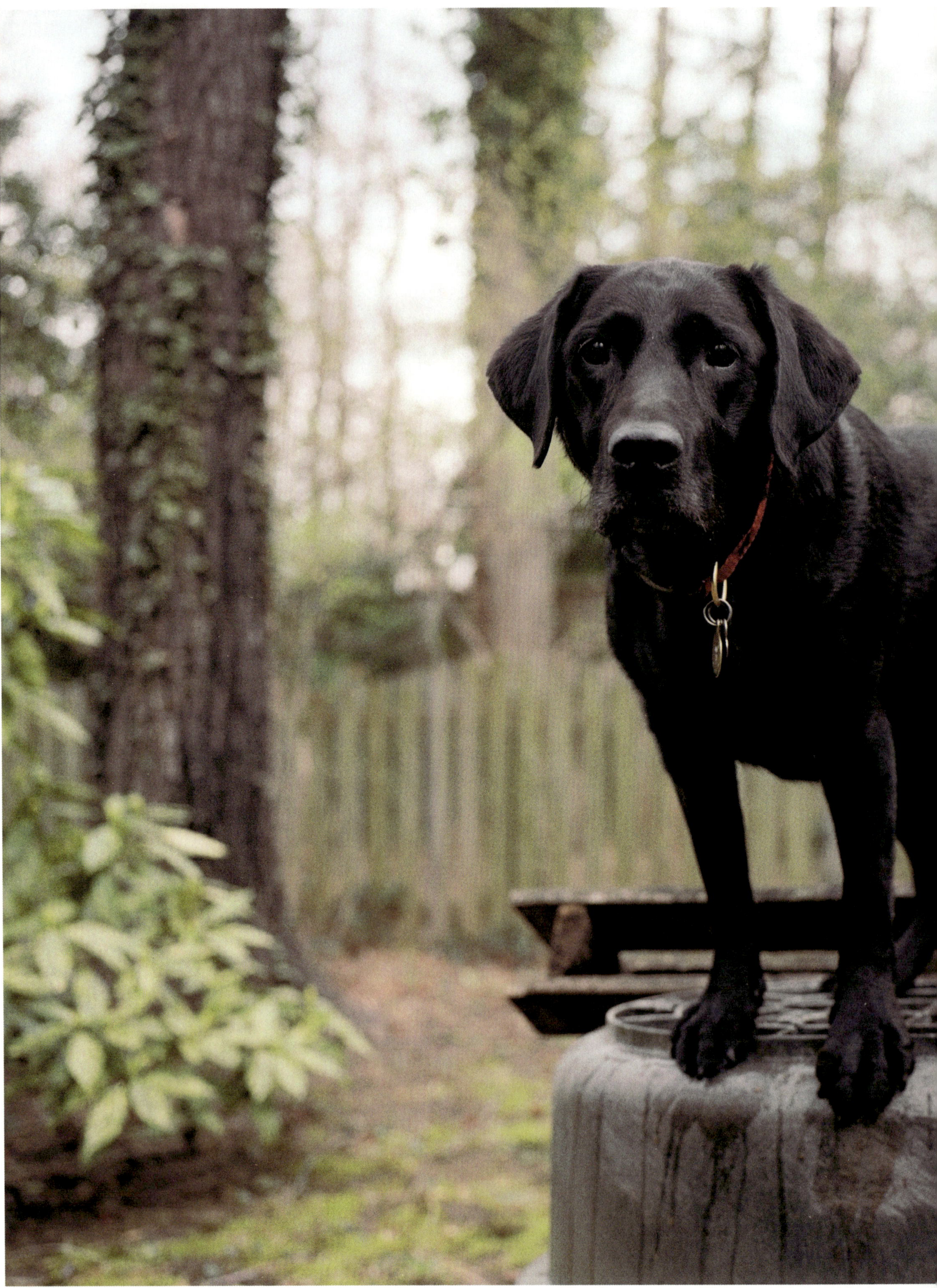

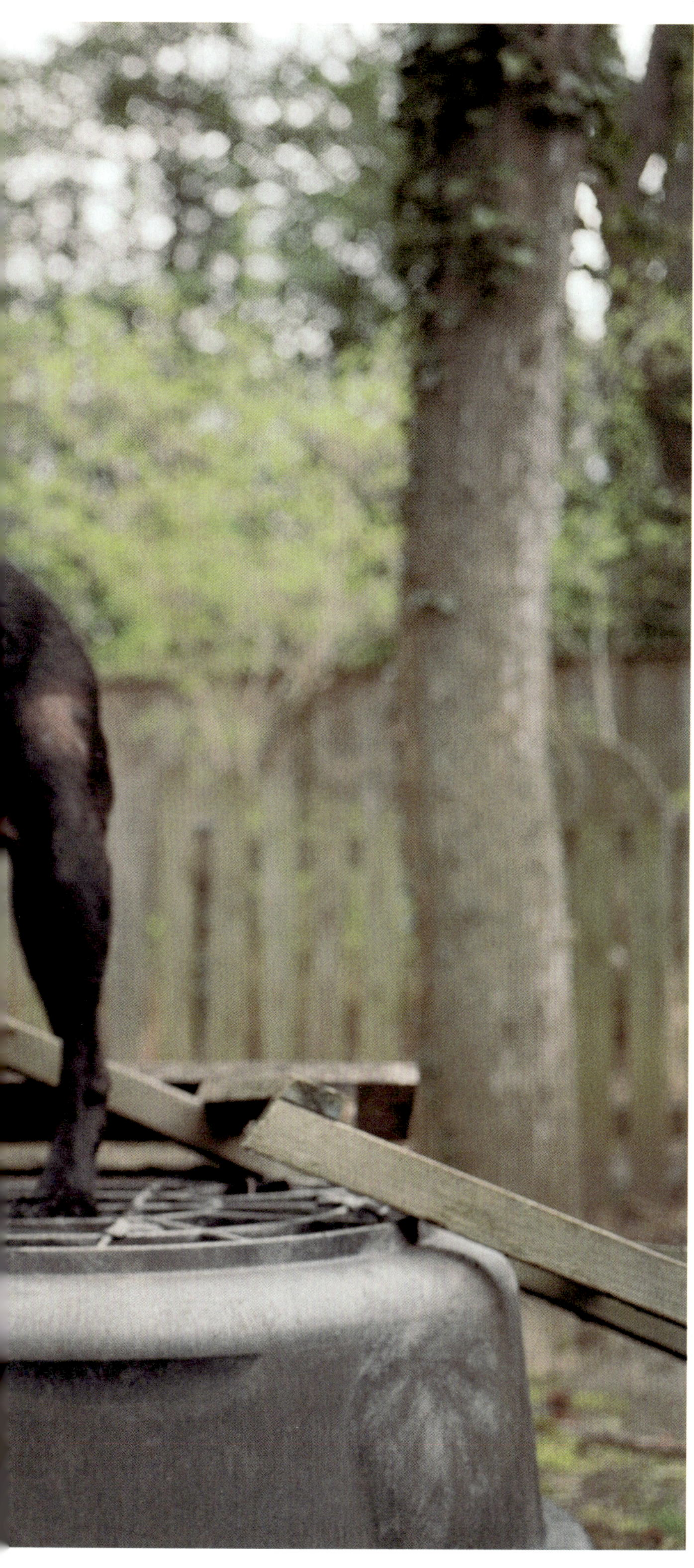

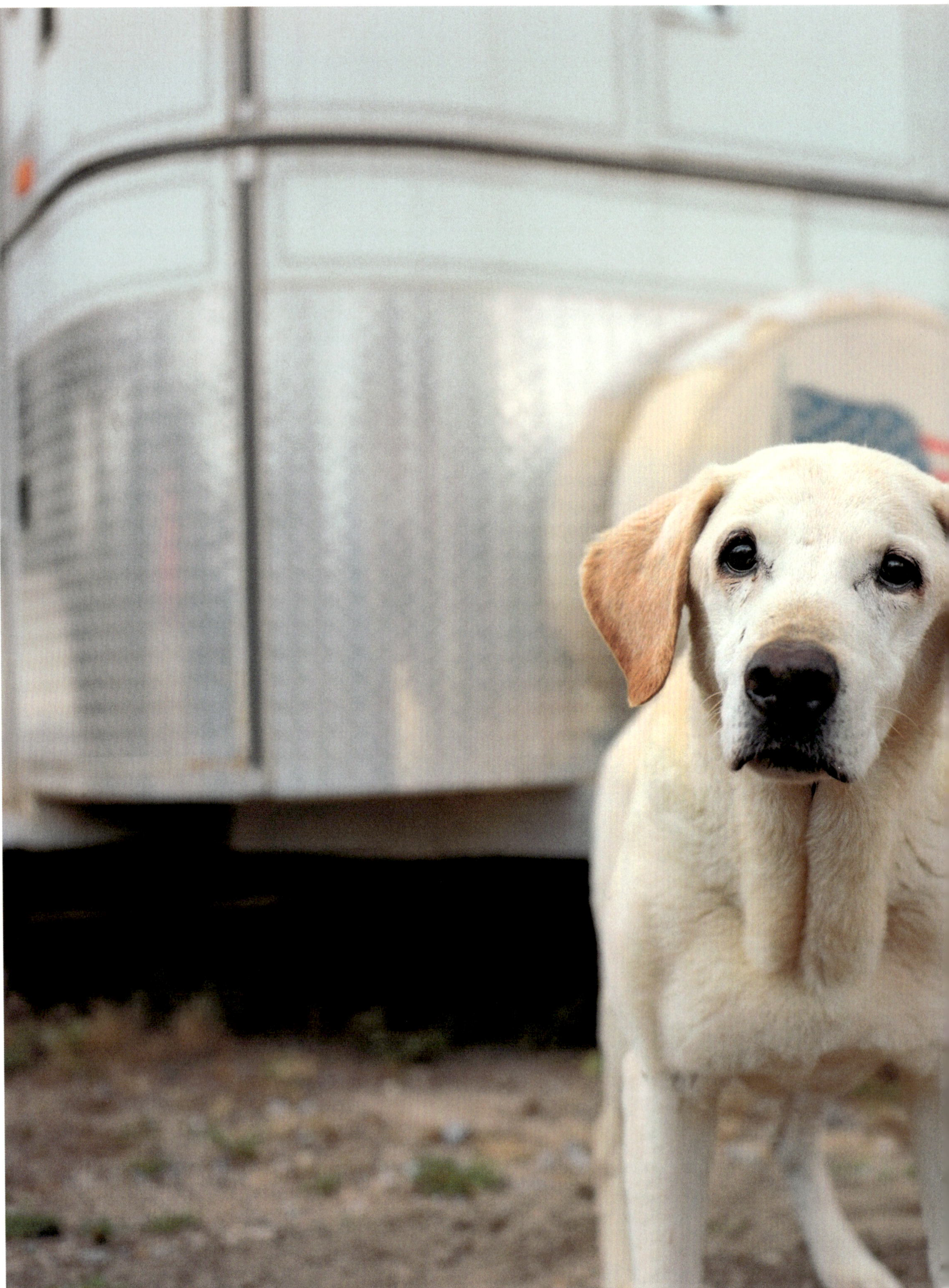

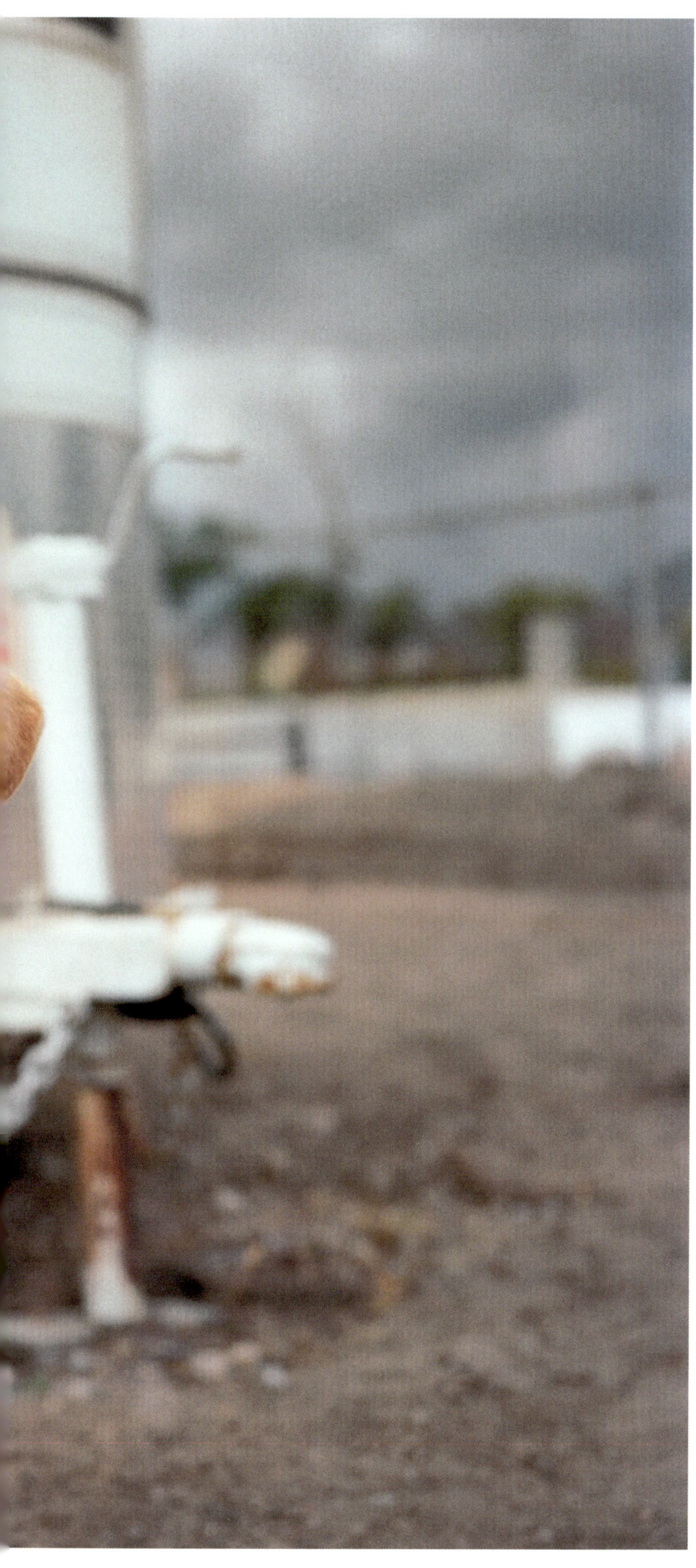

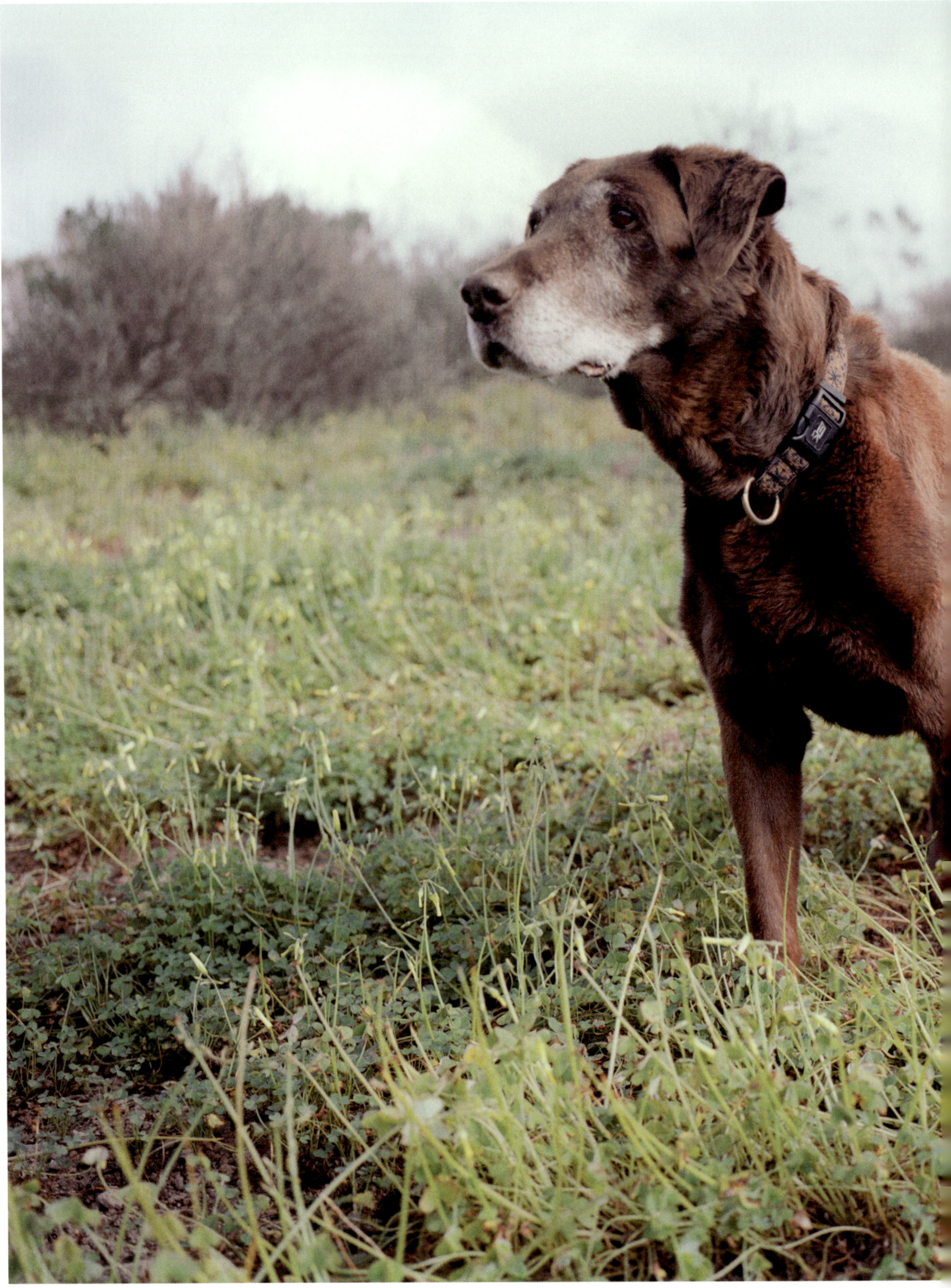

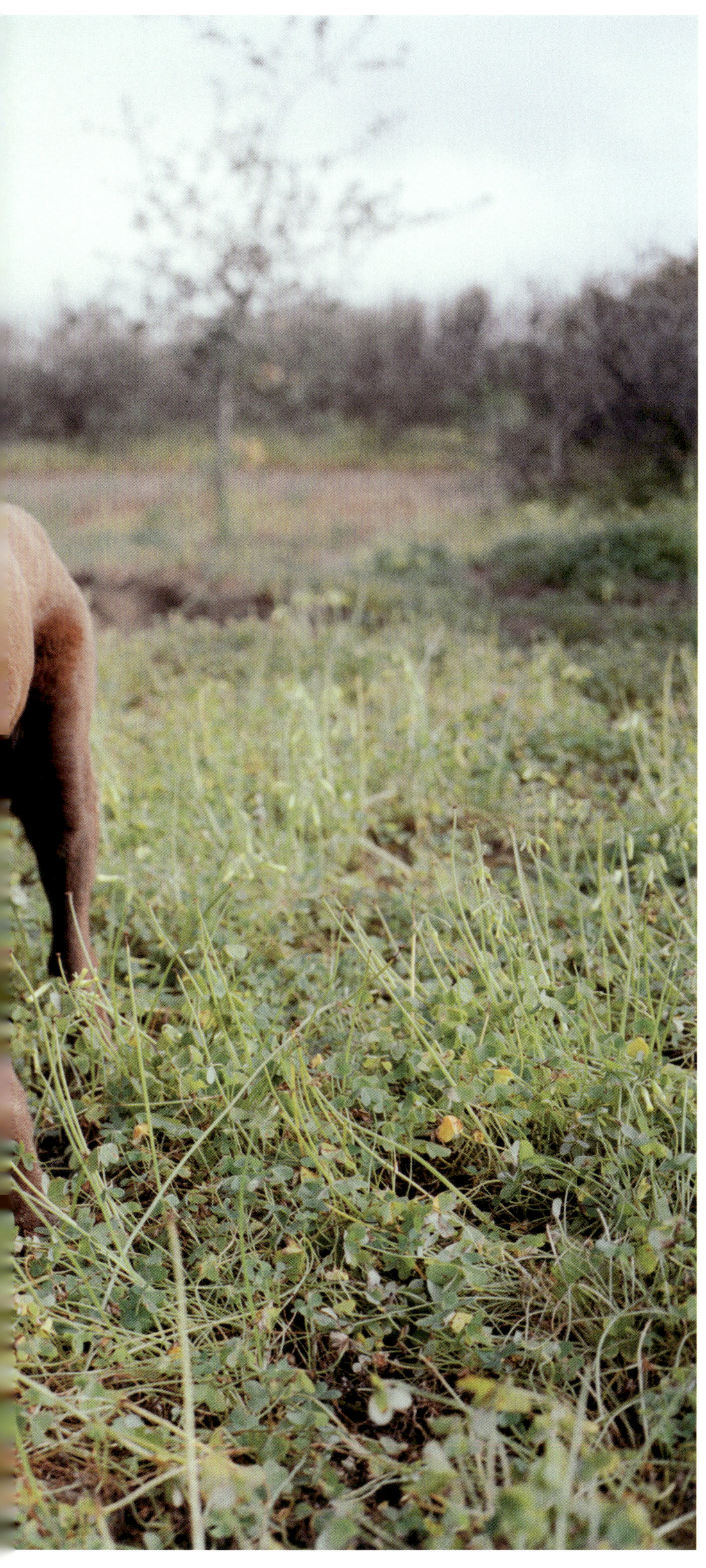

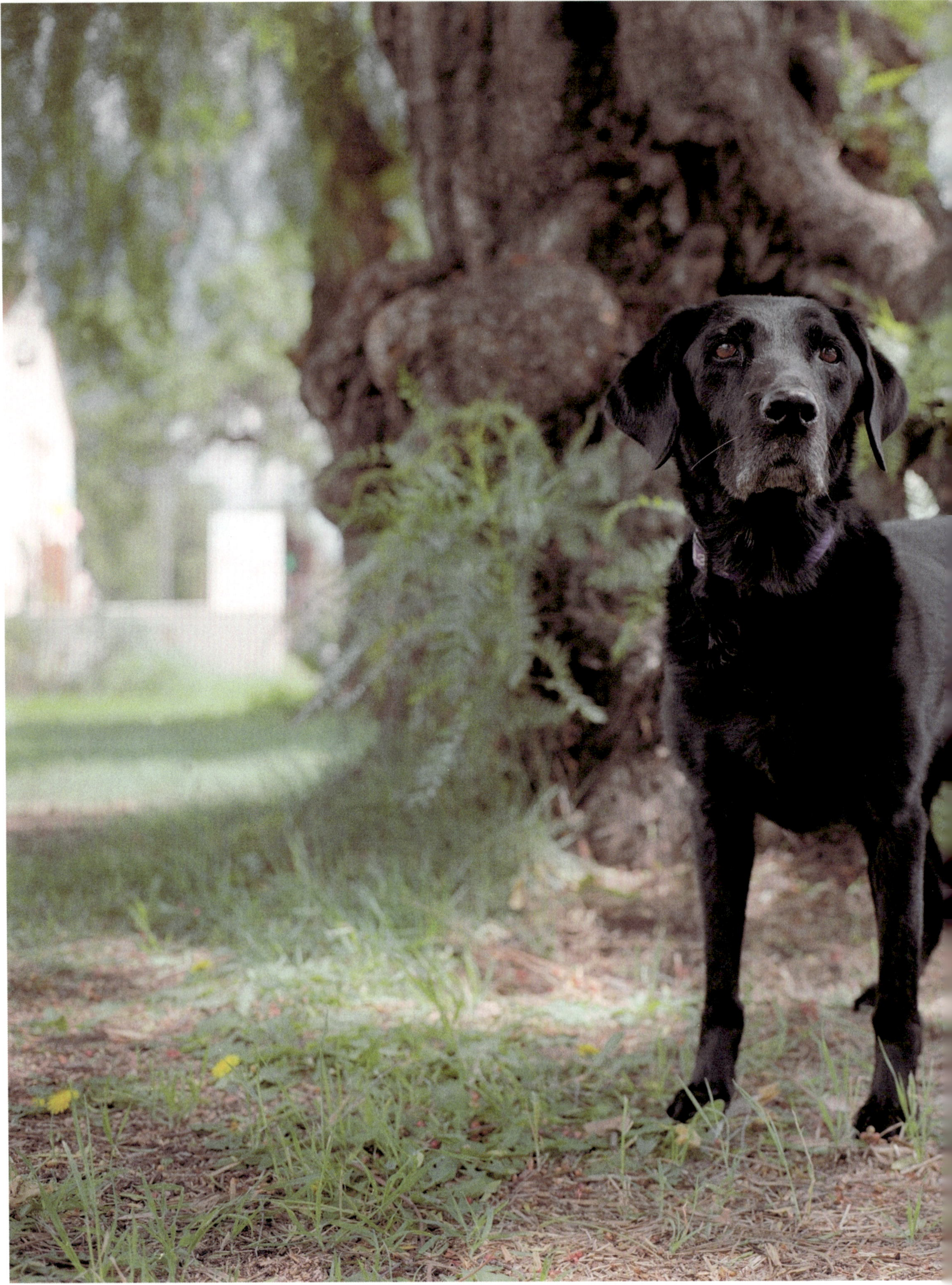

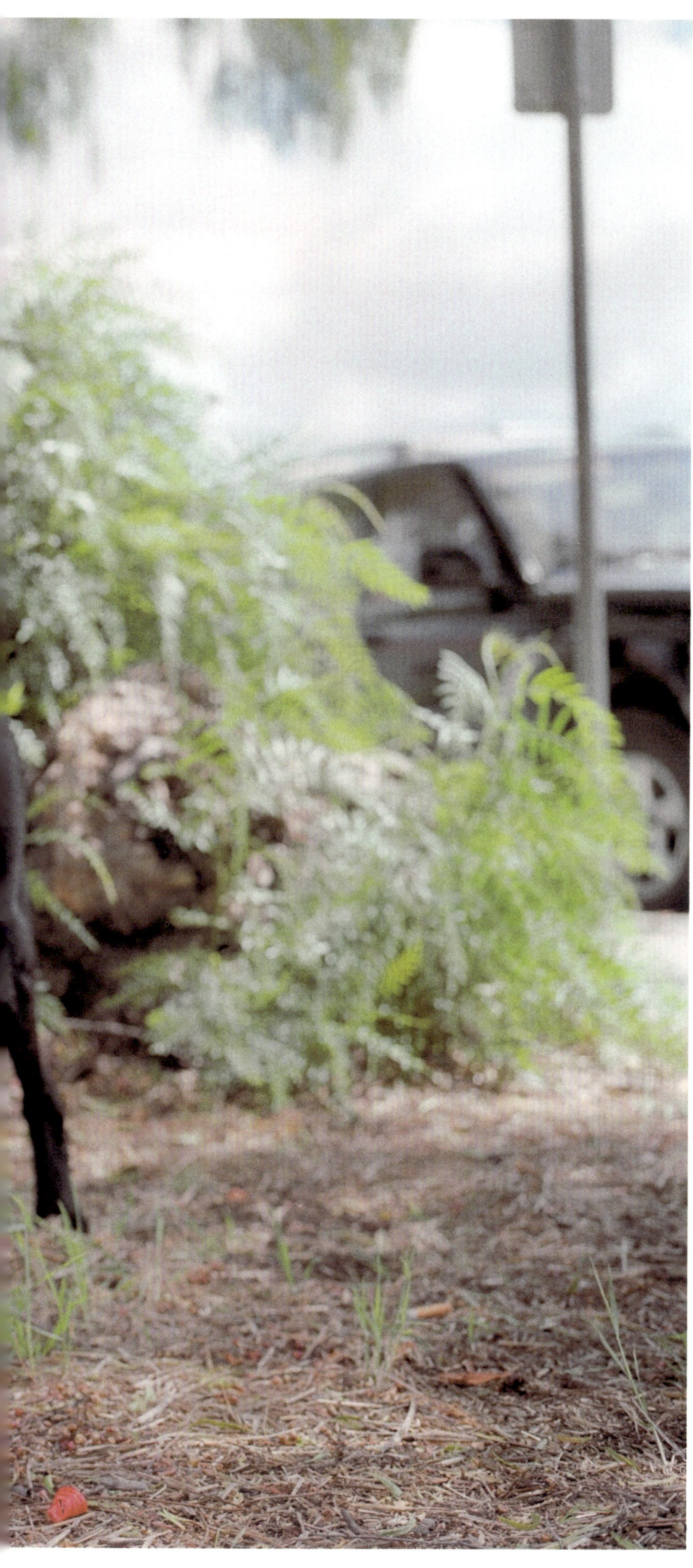

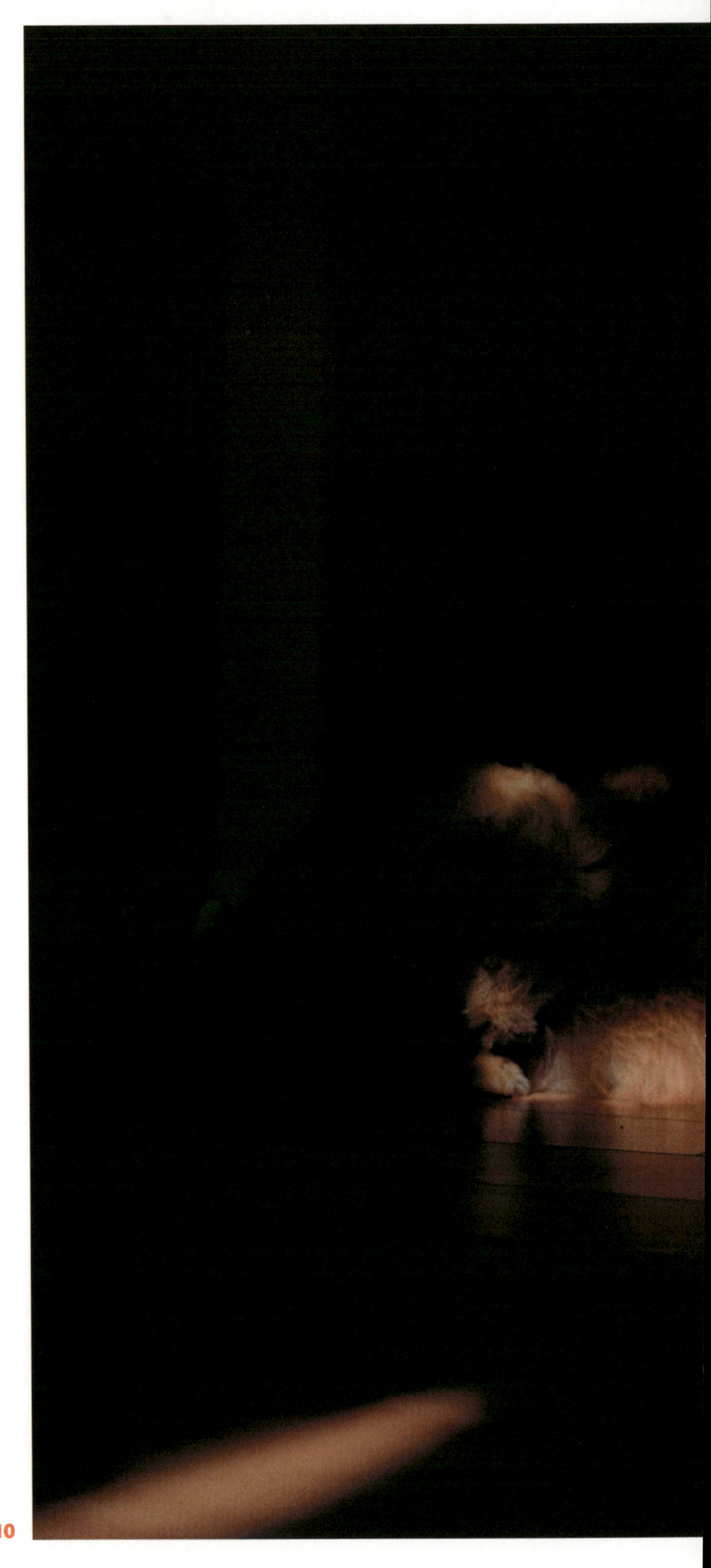

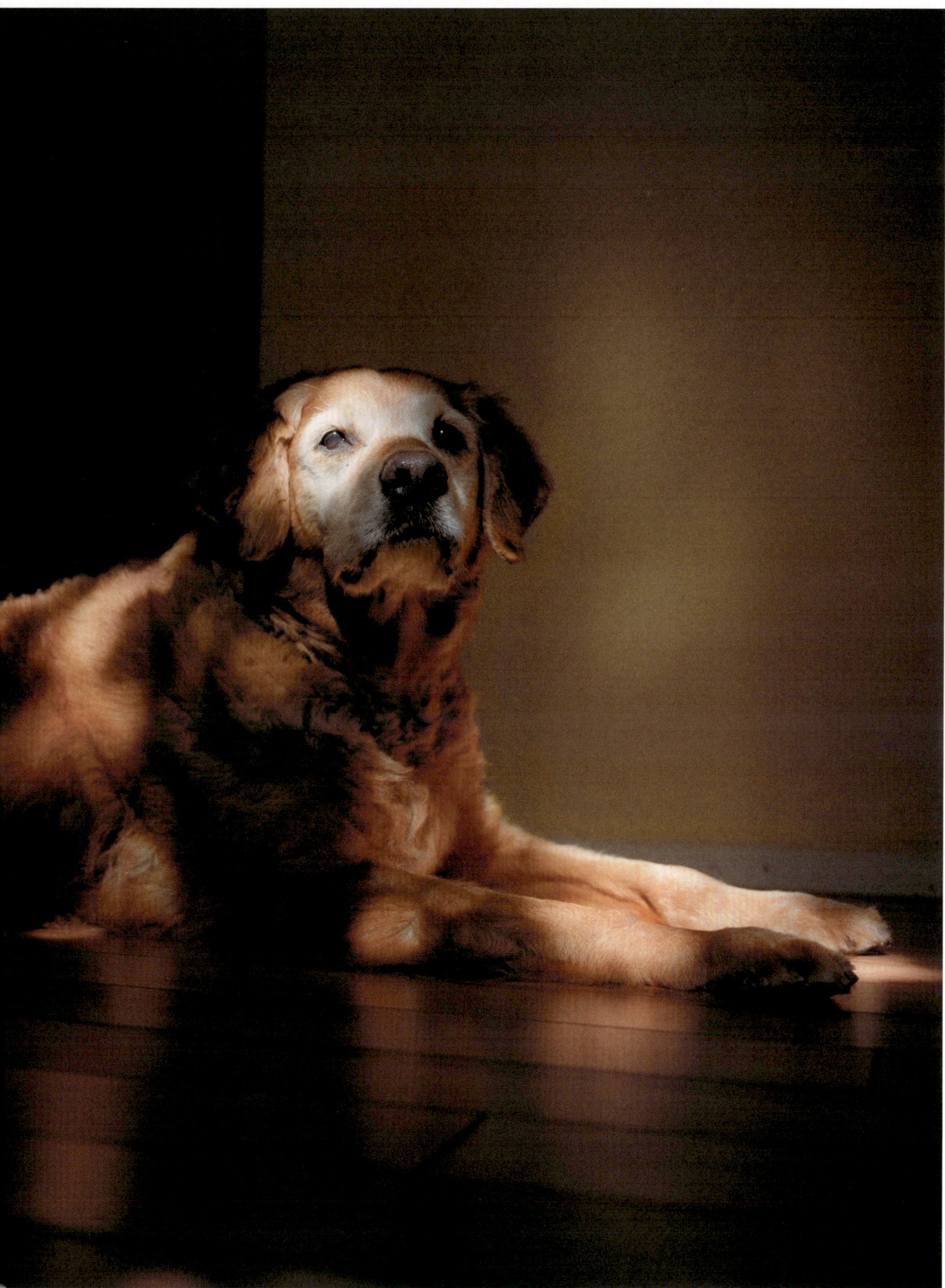

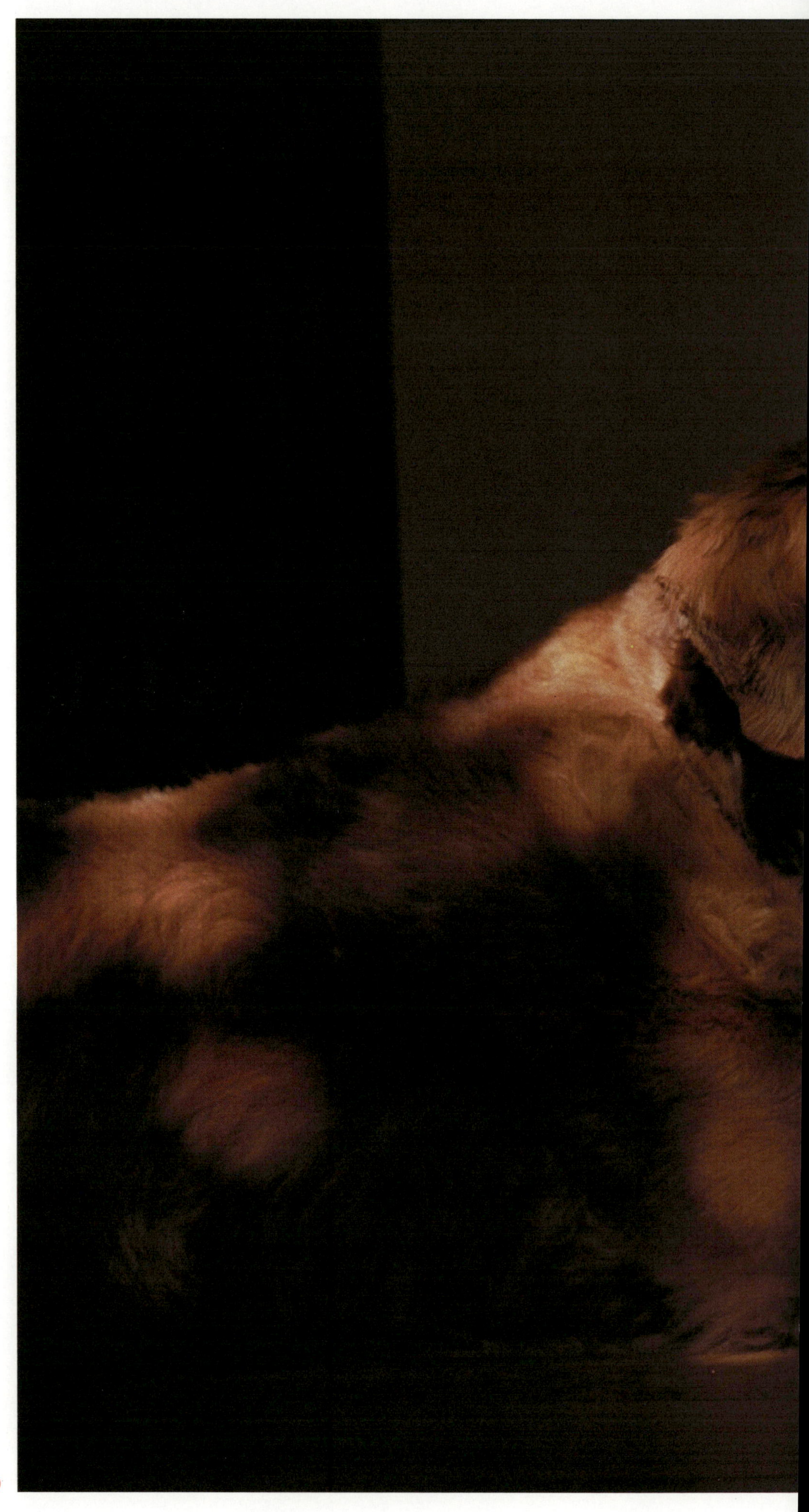

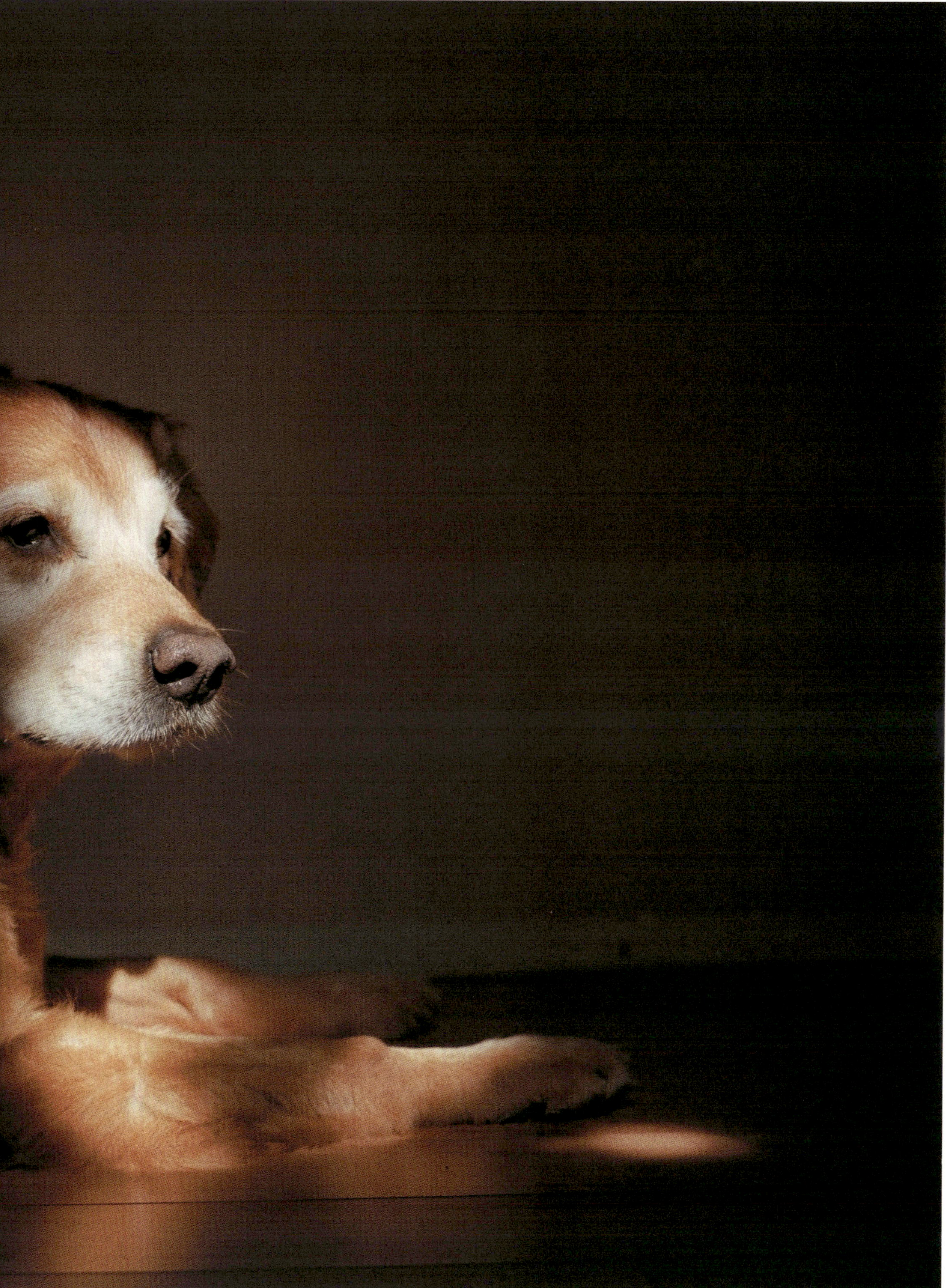

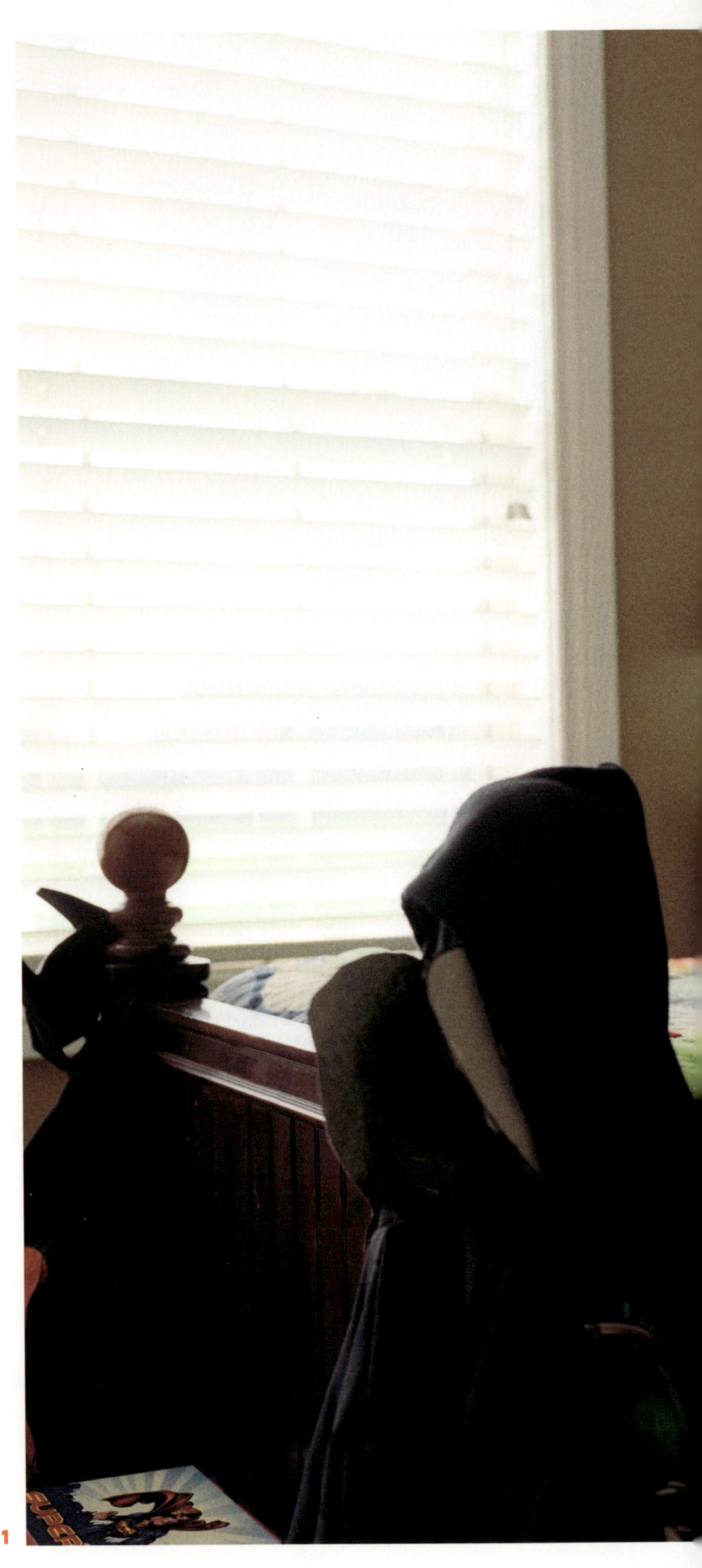

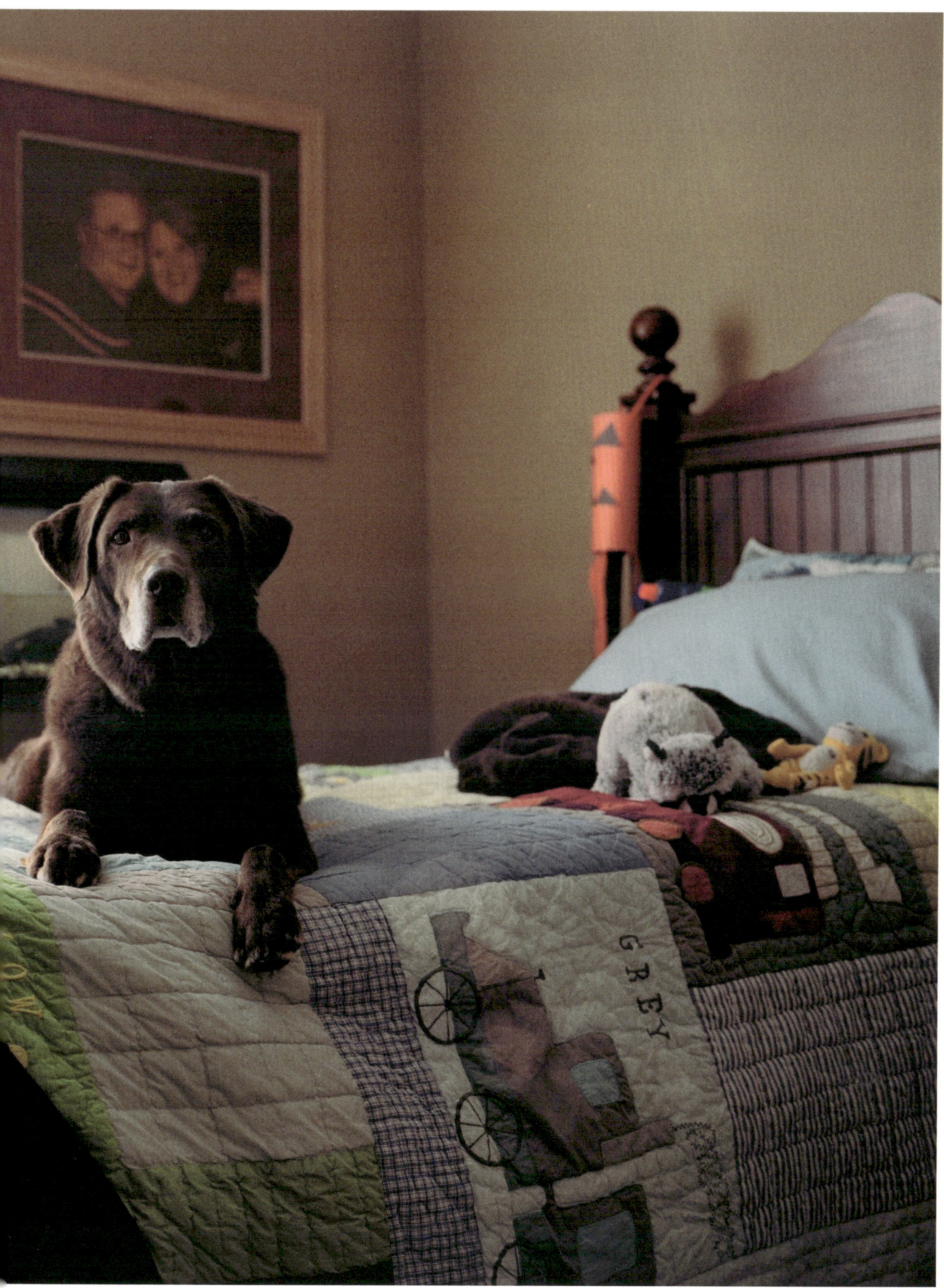
GREY

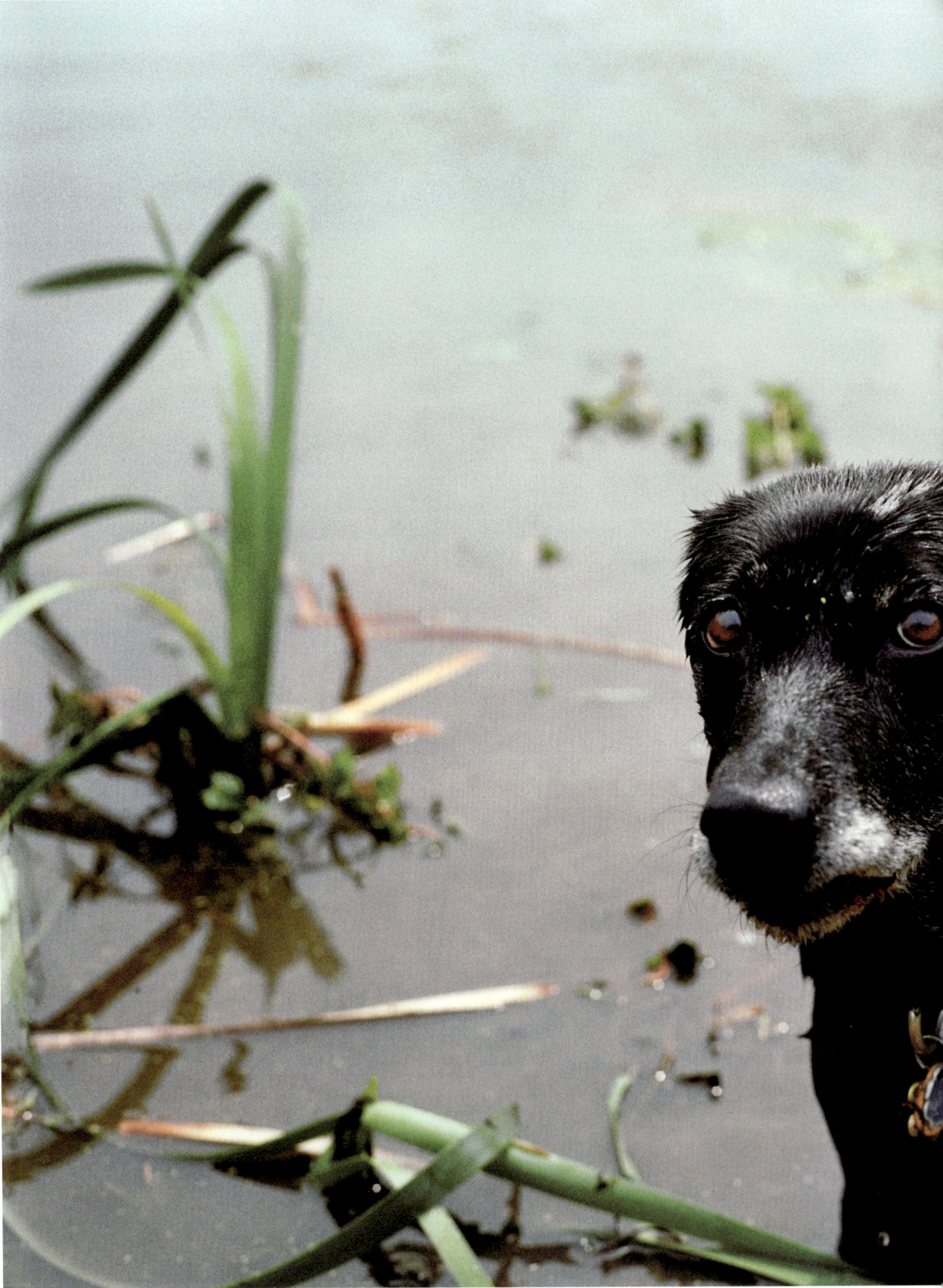

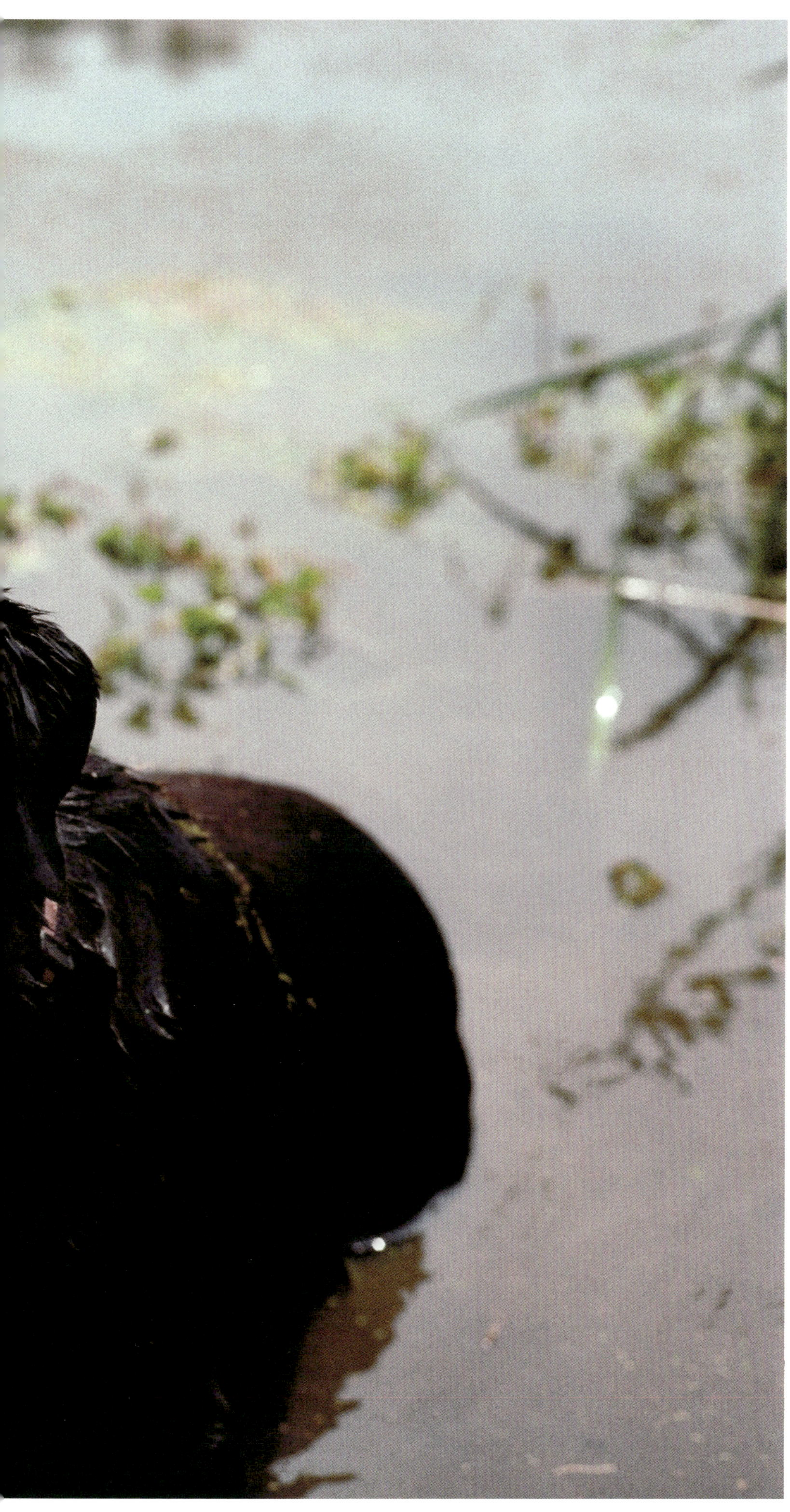

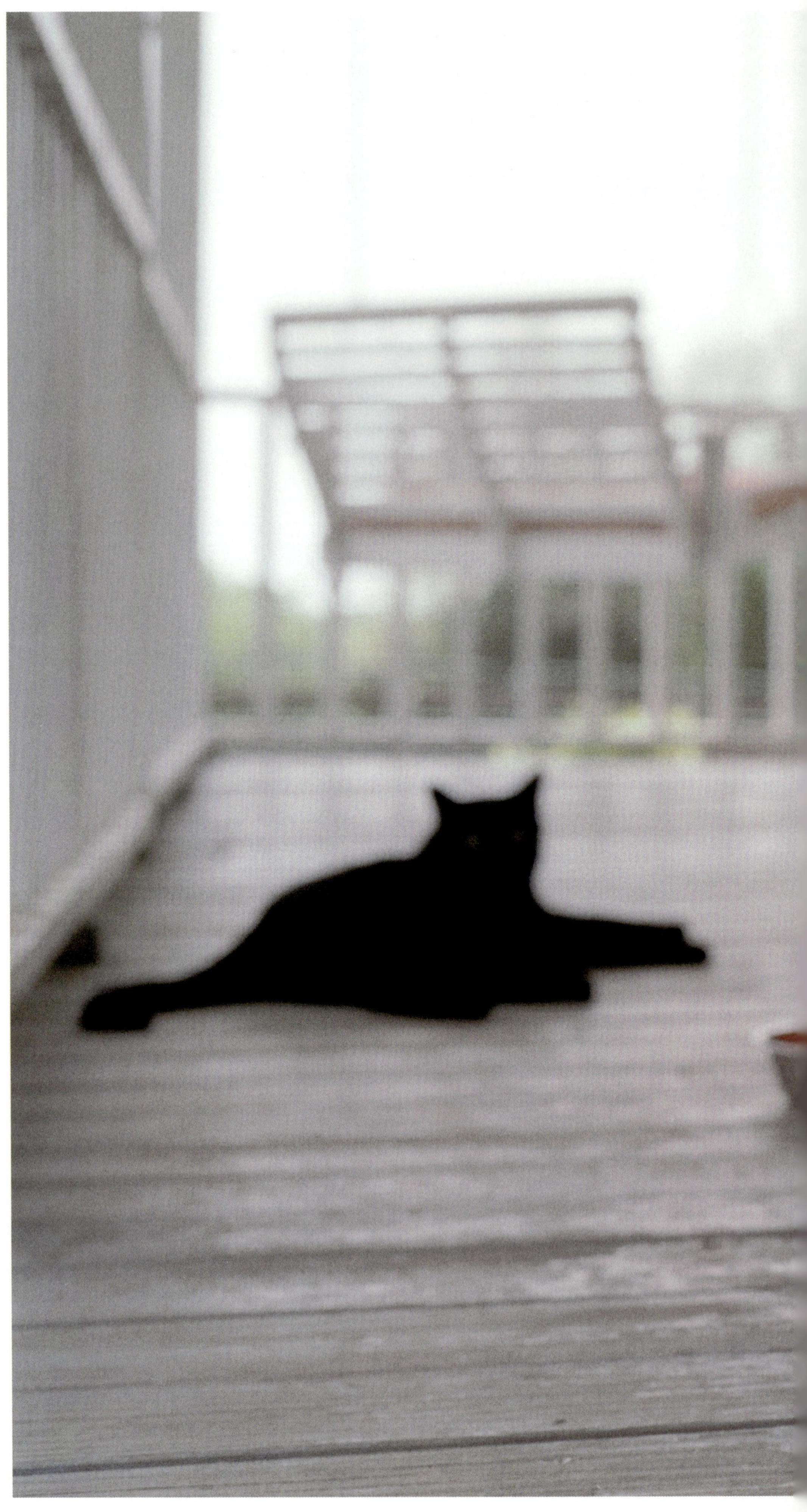

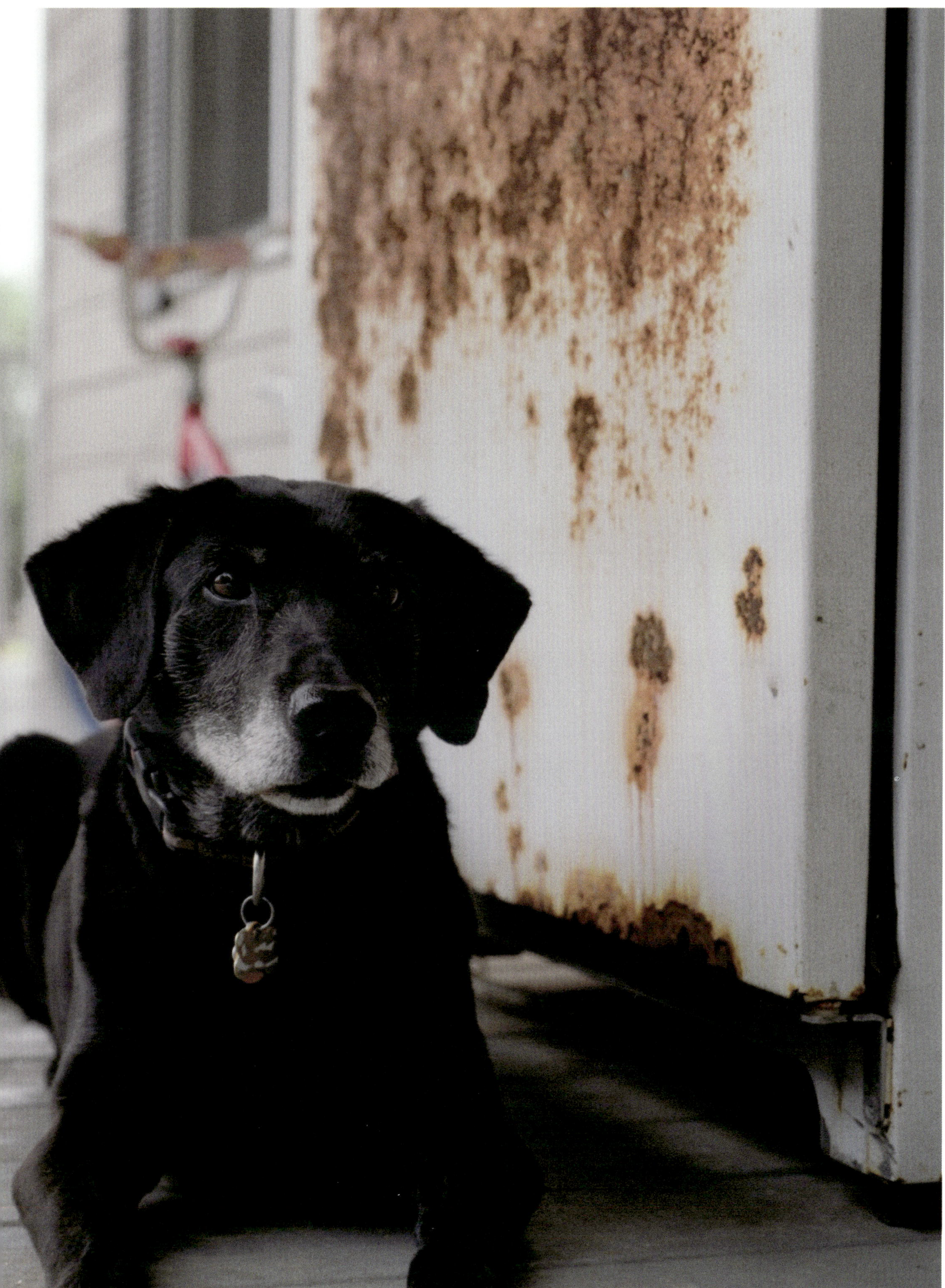

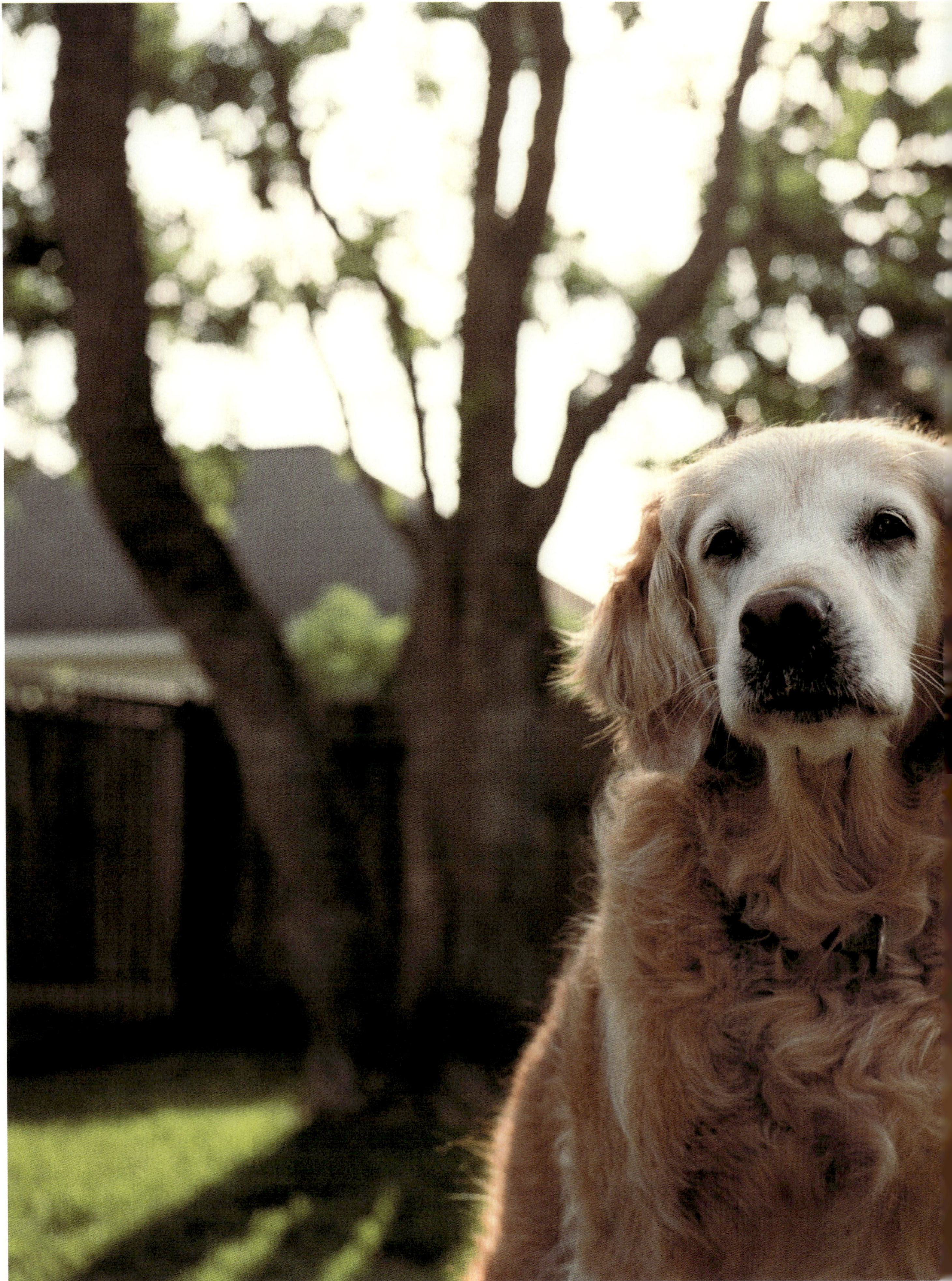

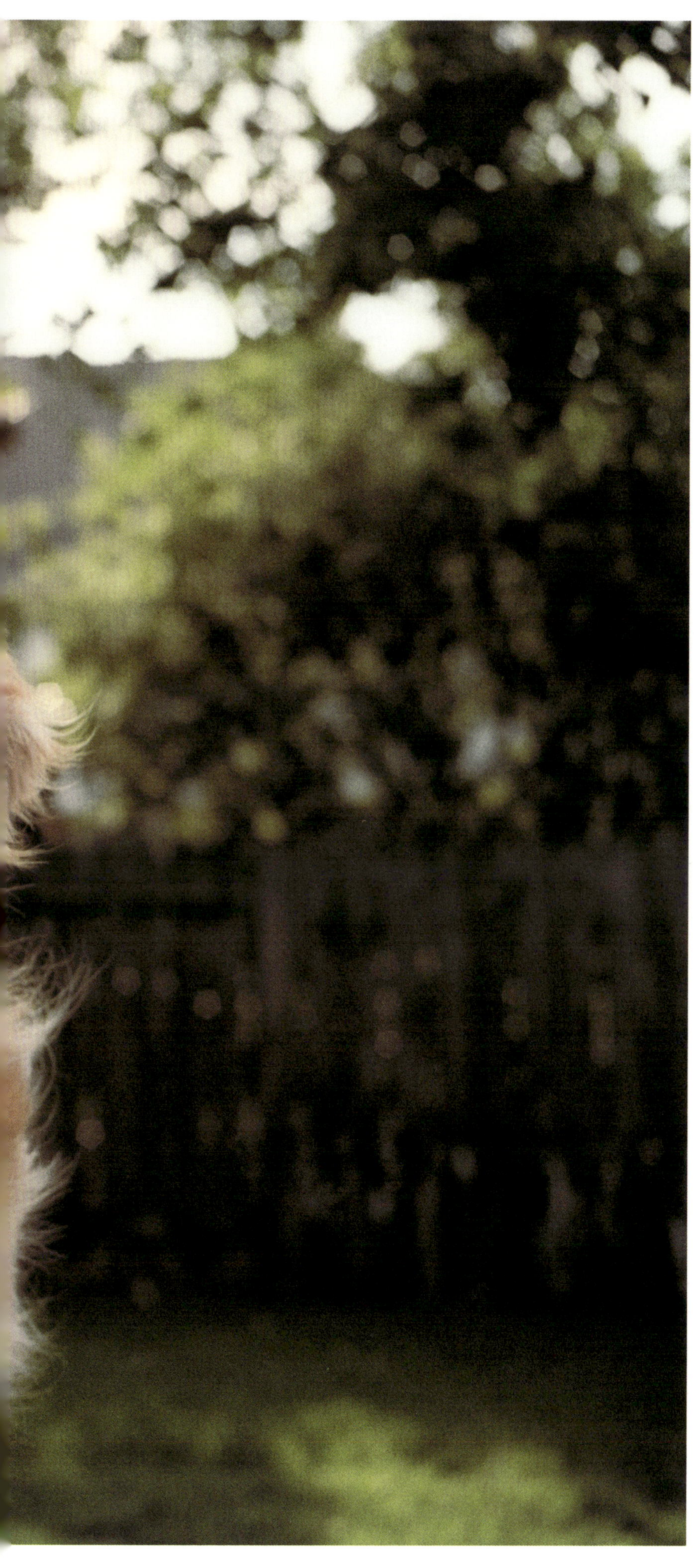

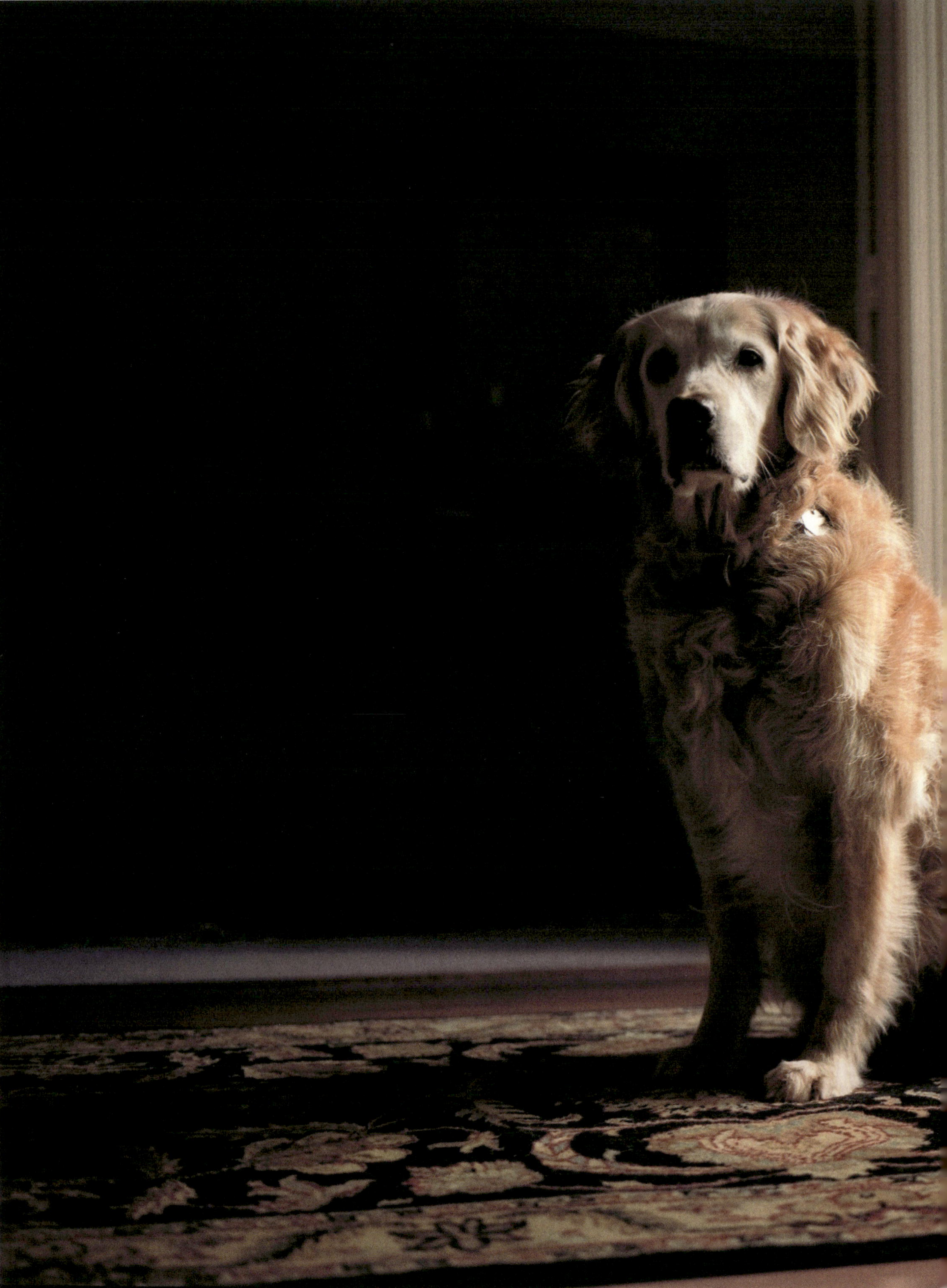

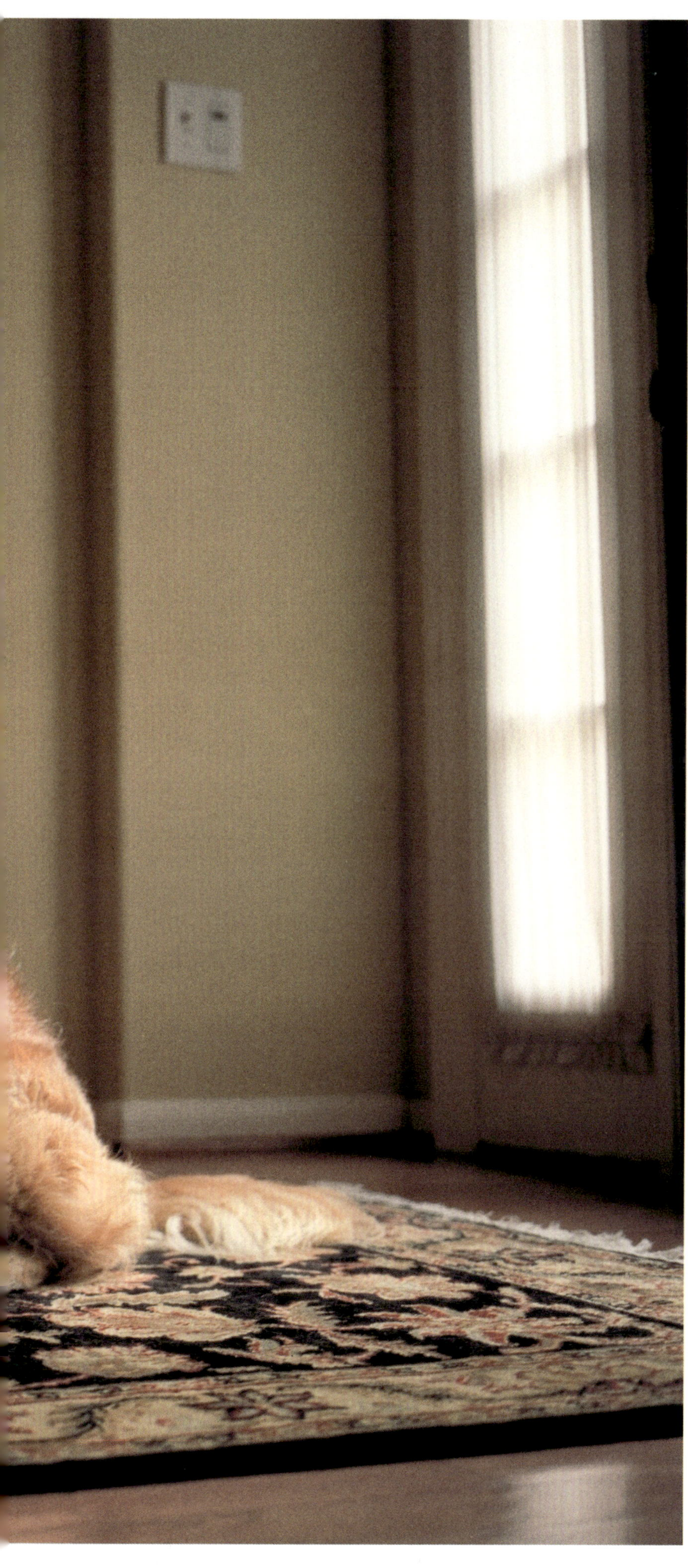

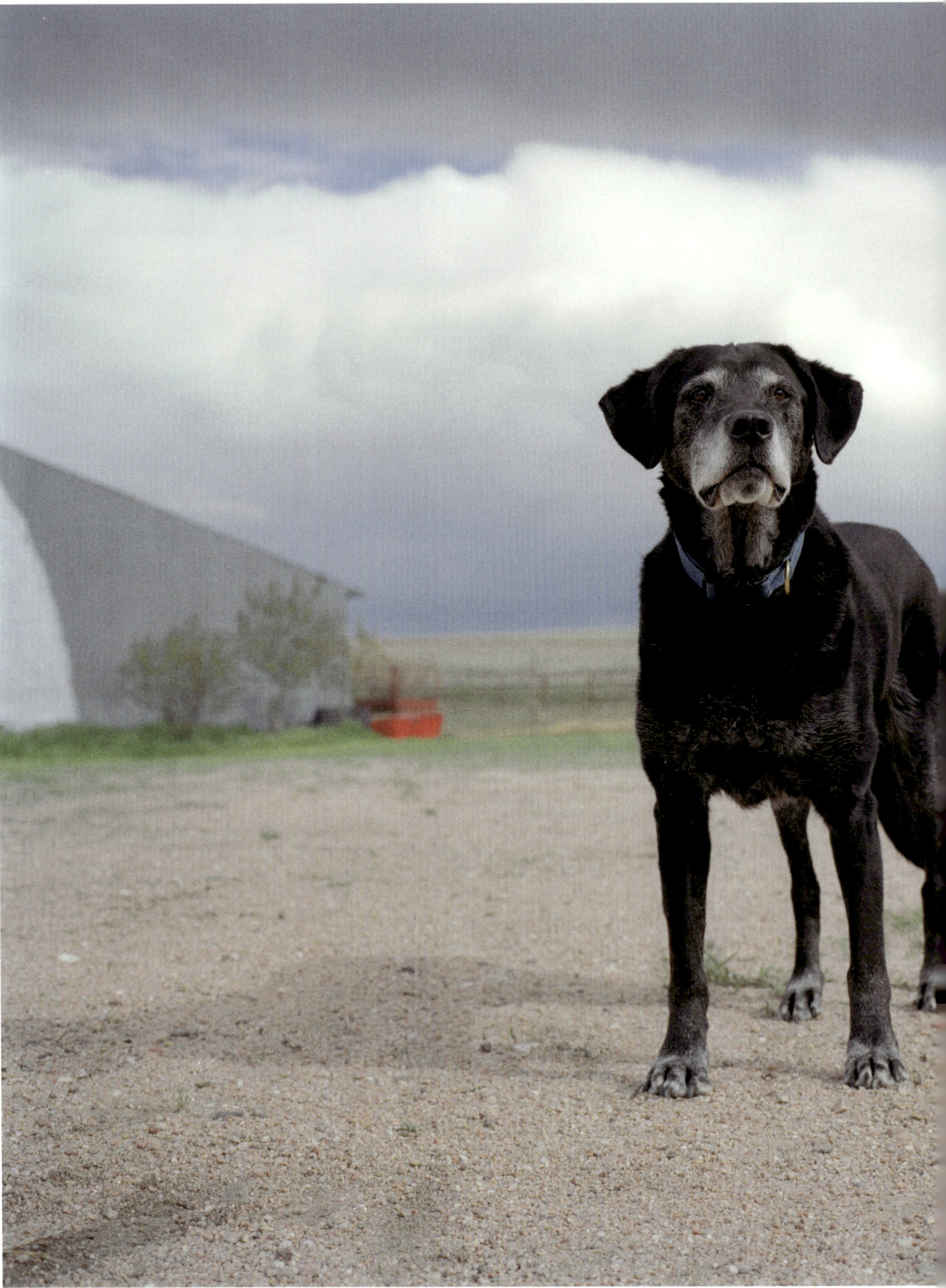

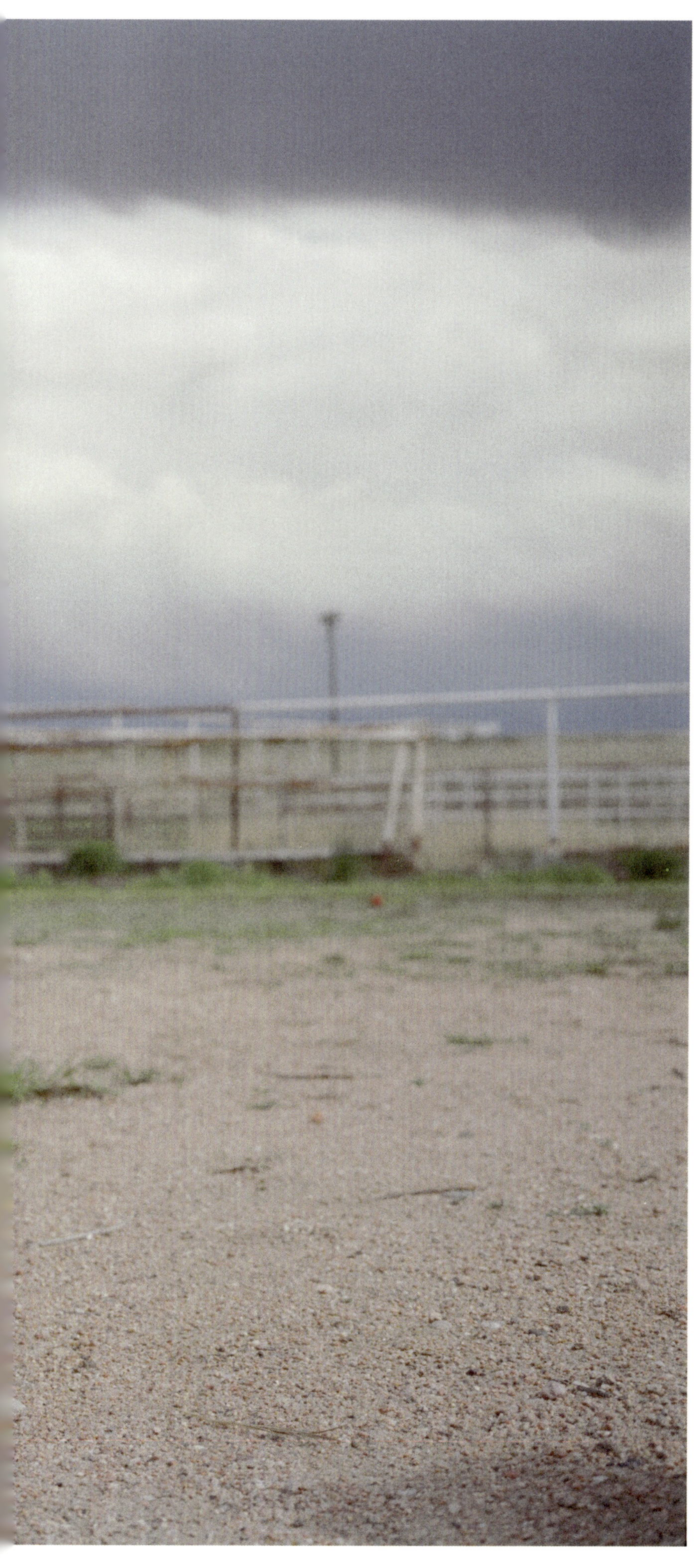

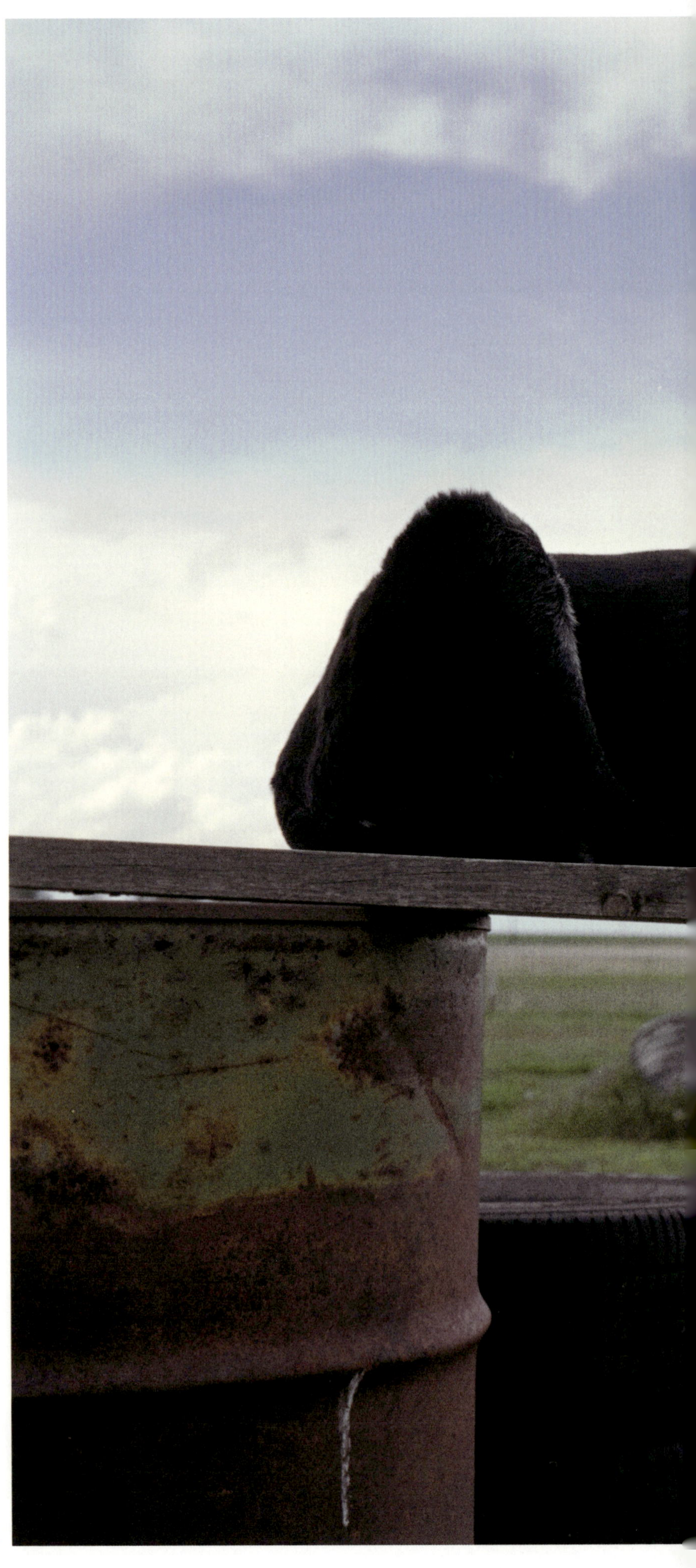

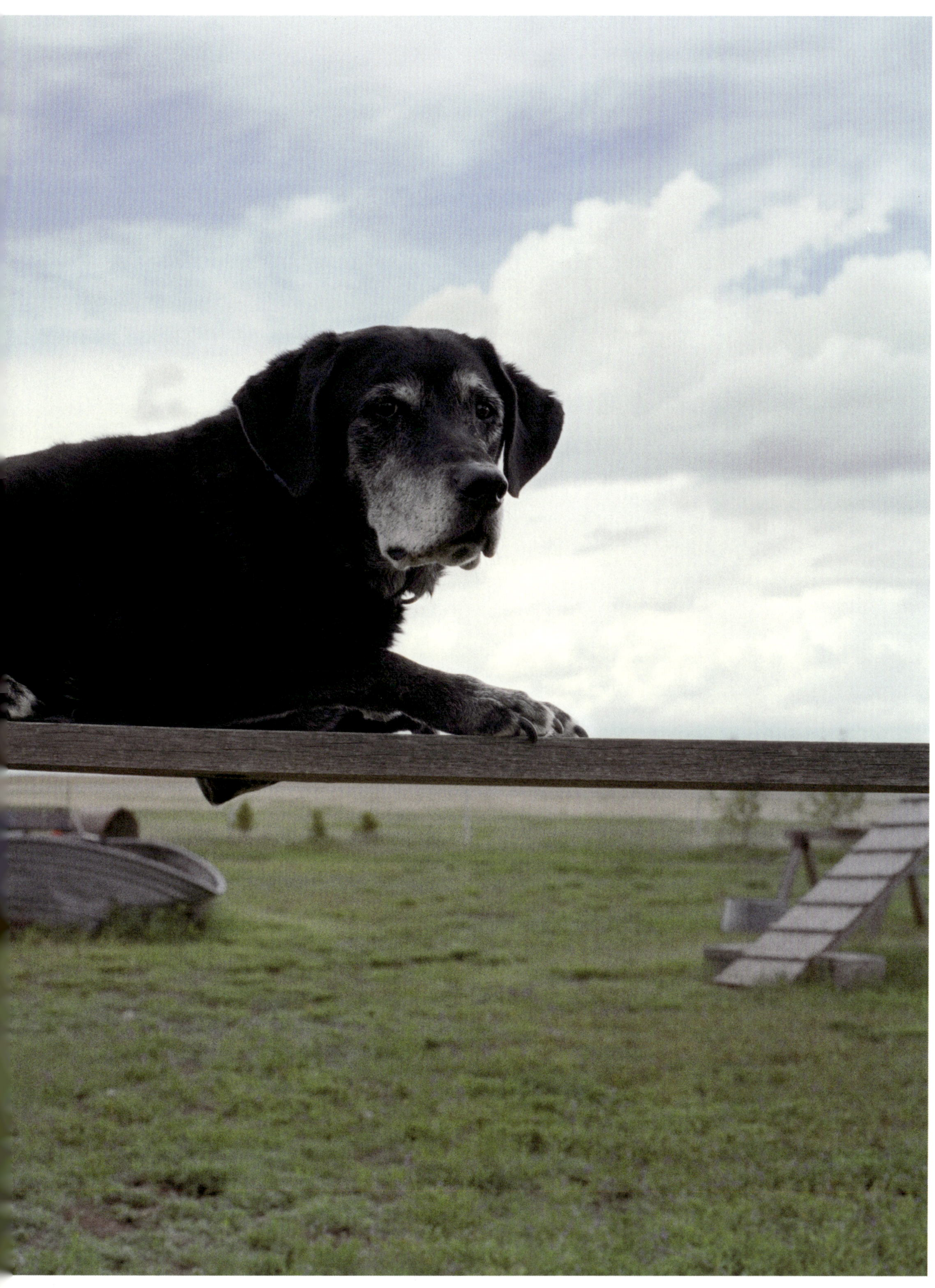

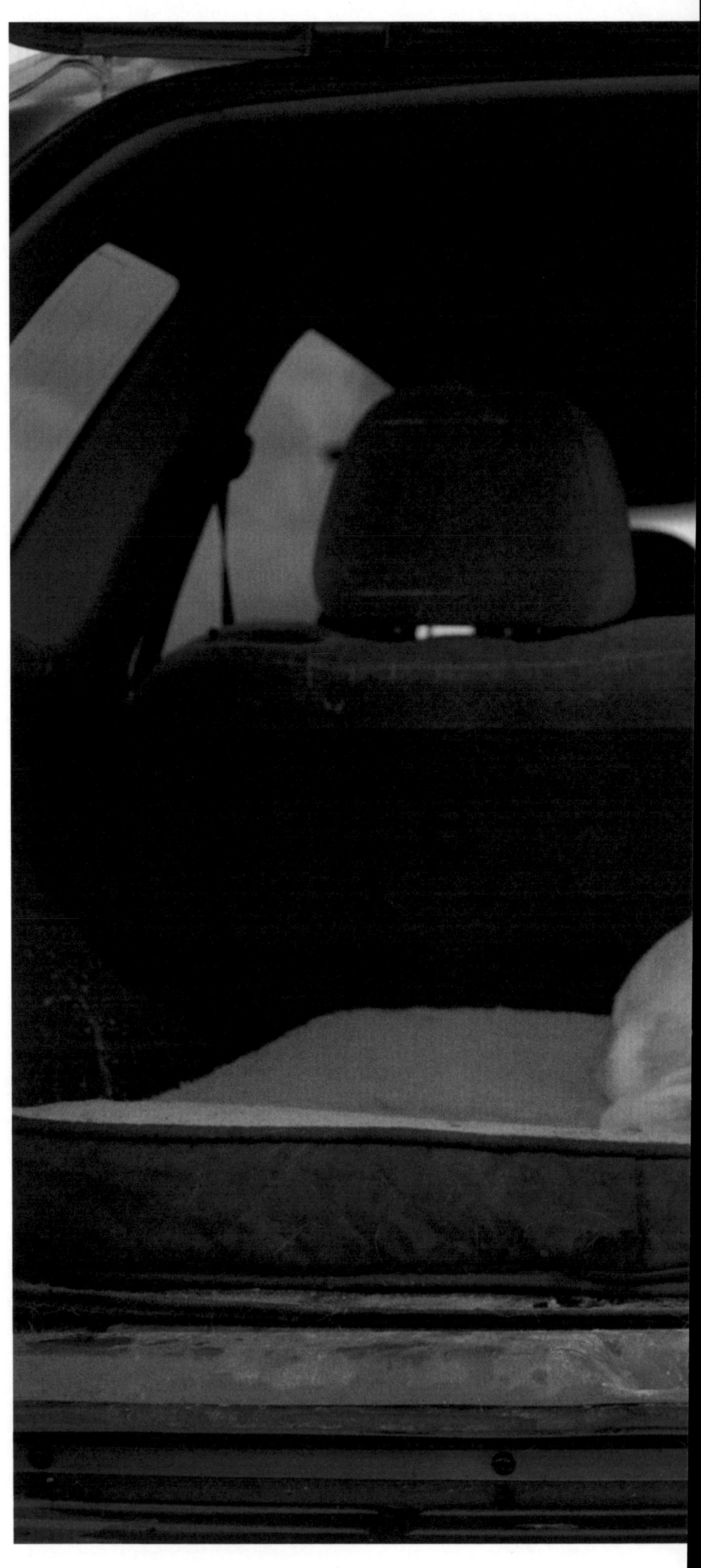

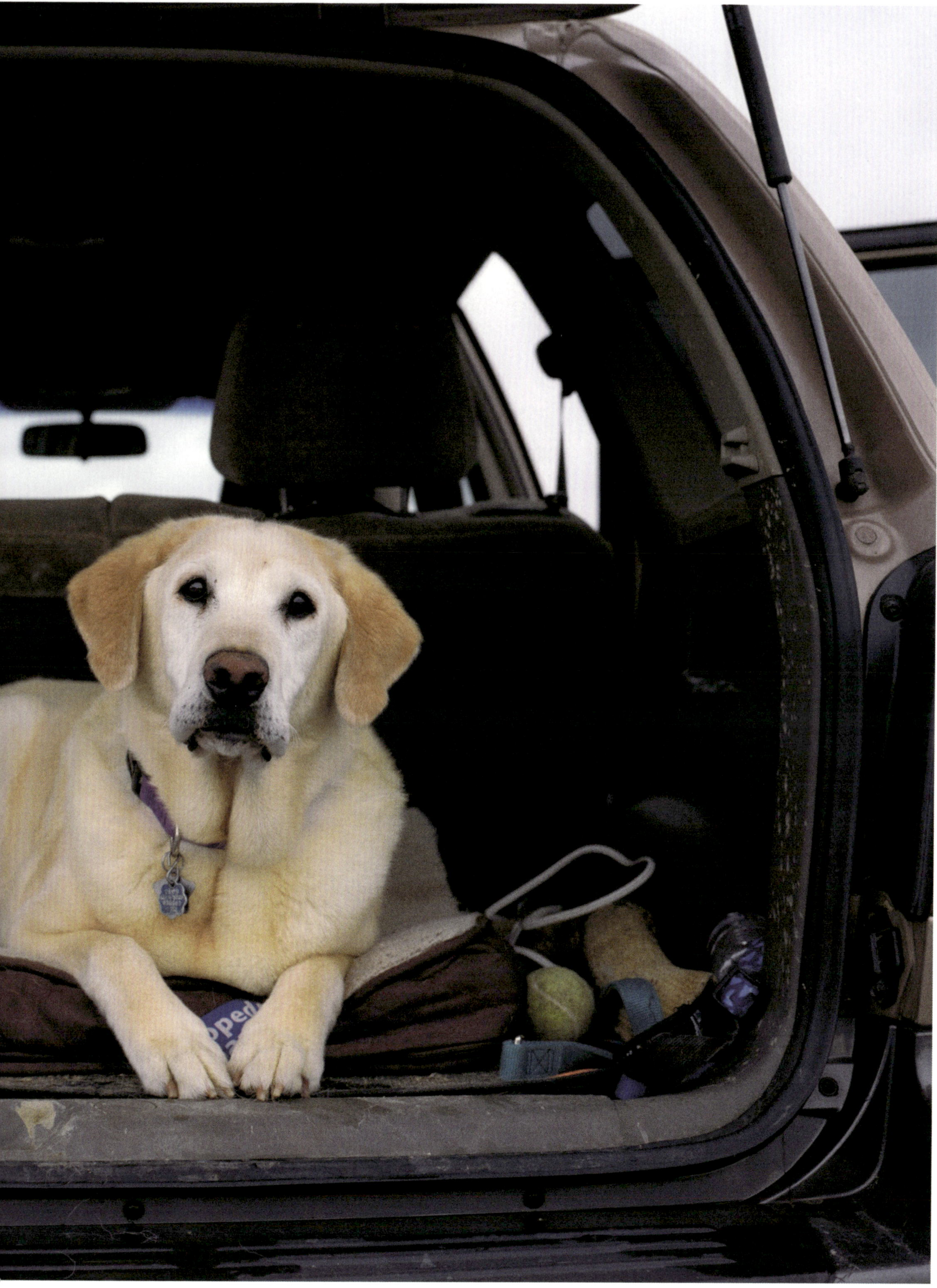

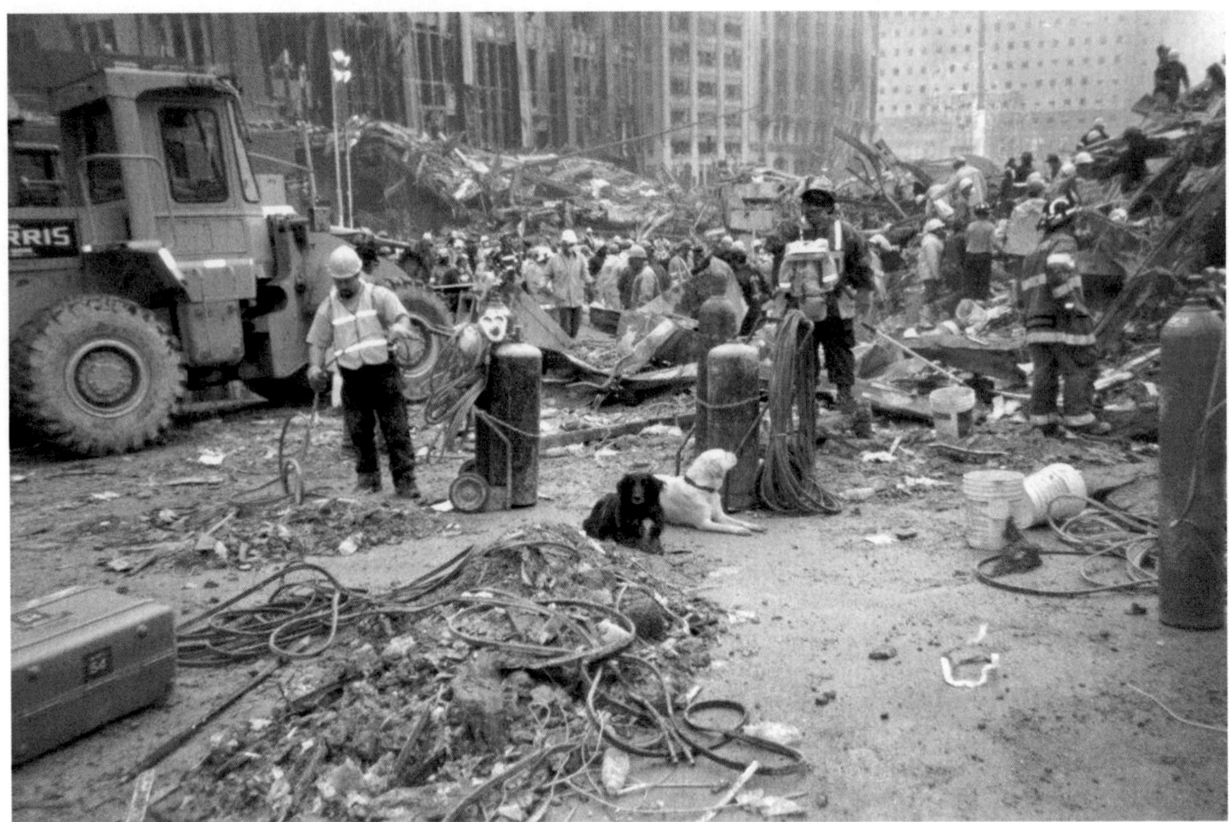

Scout and Polly at the WTC in 2001 during a 'long down,' waiting for their handlers Blake Wallis and Marti Vanada to return.
photo Blake Wallis

RETRIEVED

On and after September 11, 2001, the Federal Emergency Management Agency (FEMA) deployed close to a hundred search dogs along with their handlers—from a network of 26 active task forces from 18 different states—to both the World Trade Center in New York City and the Pentagon in Washington, D.C. In the aftermath of the attacks the dogs searched day and night for survivors, making sure no one would be stranded in the rubble, while rescue workers and firemen slowly made their way through the chaos and debris.

In my memory, the photographs of these dogs that appeared in the newspapers stayed with me most strongly: a dog being transported in a stokes basket on cables suspended high over the wreckage; another dog intently searching while maneuvering over enormous bent beams; dogs receiving eye drops after and in between shifts. I can still recall these images clearly. The dogs searched and comforted, they gave consolation to anyone involved. Seeing these pictures, I was also comforted. They somehow emanated a spark of hope amidst this scene of destruction.

I long wondered what had become of these animals. How many of them would still be alive today, so many years after 9/11? Through FEMA, I was able to locate 15 of the surviving dogs that took part in the rescue operations. I visited and portrayed them in their homes, where they all still live with their handlers across the U.S.

These animals were all at the same place at the same time, one decade ago, for the same reason: to work. That experience unites them, and was the incentive for me to pursue this subject and to photograph the dogs. They now share the vulnerability of old age while symbolizing a full decade now coming to a close.

Charlotte Dumas, August 2011

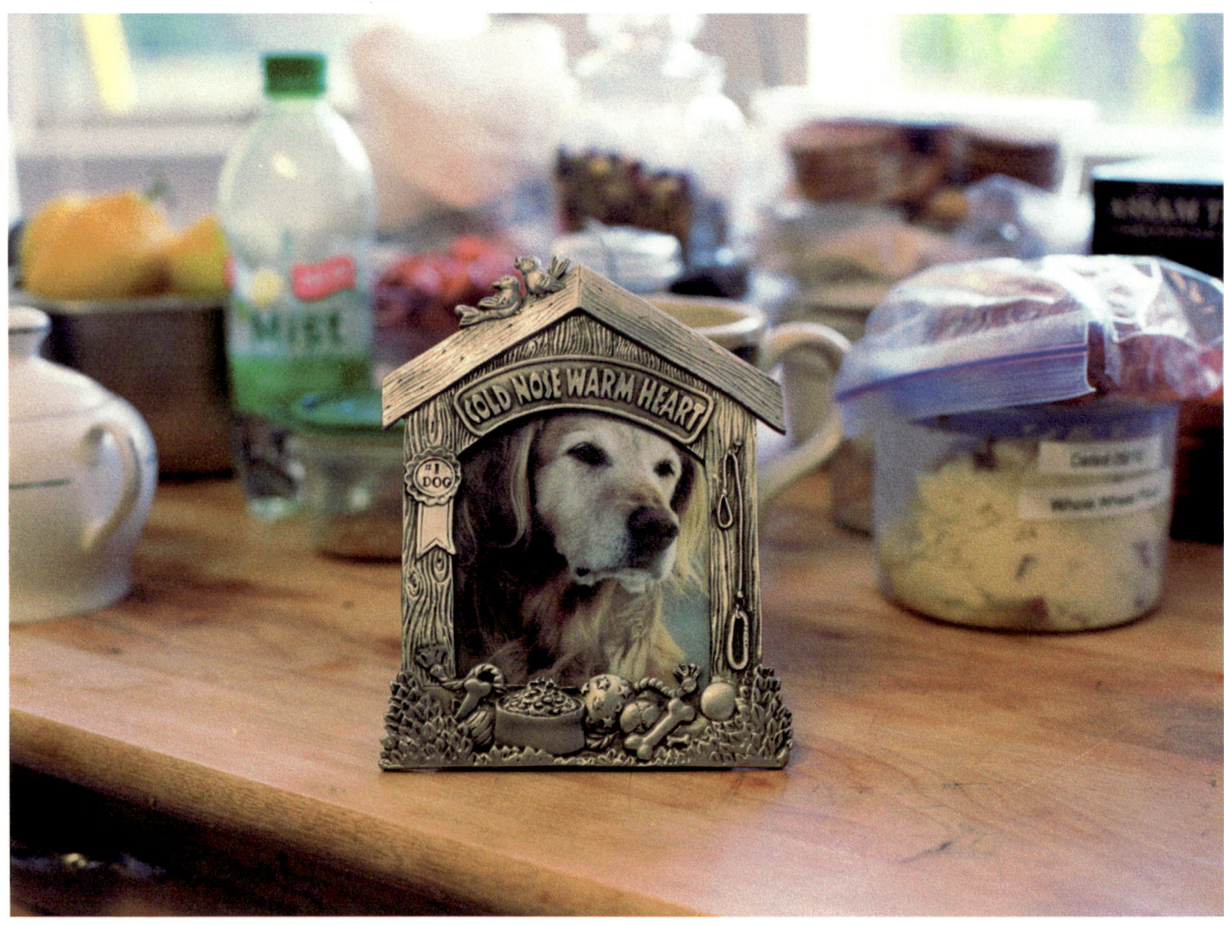

At Orion's home in Vacaville CA

THE DOGS PORTRAYED

1

MOXIE, age 13, Winthrop MA • Moxie and her handler, Mark Aliberti, arrived at the World Trade Center with MA-TF-1 on the evening of Tuesday, September 11, 2001, and searched the site for 8 days.

2

TARA, age 16, Ipswich MA • Tara and Lee Prentiss arrived at the World Trade Center with MA-TF-1 on the night of the 11th. They were there for 8 days.

3

SCOUT, age 14, McCordsville IN • IN-TF-1 was activated on the morning of the 11th. Together with Blake Wallis, Scout was deployed to the World Trade Center the same afternoon. Their last shift was on Wednesday the 19th.

4

KAISER, age 12, Indianapolis IN • Together with Tony Zintsmaster, Kaiser was deployed with IN-TF-1 to the World Trade Center on the evening of the 11th. They arrived the morning of the 12th and were on the search until the 19th.

5

RED, age 11, Annapolis MD • Red and Heather Roche were deployed to the Pentagon from September 16 until the 27th. They were part of the Bay Area Recovery Canines and later joined the MD-TF-1.

6

GABRIEL, age 12, Rhoadesville VA • Gabriel and Lisa Berry were sent to the Pentagon with VA-TF-2 on the 11th and arrived that evening. They stayed for 7 days.

7

GUINNESS, age 15, Highland CA • Sheila McKee and Guinness flew the evening of the 12th with CA-TF-6 and started working on the morning of the 13th. They were deployed to the World Trade Center for 11 days.

8

DUKE, age 14, Thousand Oaks CA • Duke and Howard Orr arrived with CA-TF-8 at the World Trade Center on September 17 and were deployed for 10 days.

9

ABIGAIL, age 13, Ojai CA • Abigail and Debra Tosch were deployed together with Duke and Howard Orr, arriving on the evening of September 17 at the World Trade Center and then searching for 10 days.

10

ORION, age 13, Vacaville CA • Orion and Robert Macaulay were part of the third wave of deployments and worked with the CA-TF-4 at the World Trade Center from September 23 to October 1.

11

TUFF, age 12, Ashland MO • Tuff and Tom Andert arrived in New Jersey with the MO-TF-1 at 11:00 pm on the 11th to start working early the next day the World Trade Center.

12

BAILEY, age 14, Franklin TN • Bailey and Keith Lindley were deployed to the Pentagon with TN-TF-1. They arrived the morning of the 12th and searched for 9 days.

13

BRETAGNE, age 13, Cypress TX • Denise Corliss and Bretagne were at the World Trade Center from September 17 to the 27th with TX-TF-1.

14

MERLYN, age 14, Otis CO • Merlyn, owned by Ann Wichmann, was deployed with handler Matt Claussen and worked the night shift while Ann and search dog Jenner worked during the day as part of CO-TF-1. They searched the rubble of the World Trade Center for five days starting on September 24.

15

HOKE, age 13, Denver CO • Julie Noyes and Hoke were also part of CO-TF-1. With Julie by his side, Hoke was deployed to the World Trade Center on September 24 and searched for 5 days.

RETRIEVED

This book is dedicated to all search dogs that save lives
and provide comfort and consolation in times of distress.
And to Avis, who loves dogs.

Since the initial publication the names of several more surviving search dogs
of the 9/11 rescue operations have come to my attention.
I would like to acknowledge them here: Atos, Woody, Jessie, Tosca and Smokey.

MANY THANKS
Teresa MacPherson at FEMA, Celeste Matesevac at the NDSDF, Lee Prentiss, Mark Aliberti, Blake Wallis, Tony Zintsmaster, Heather Roche, Lisa Berry, Sheila McKee, Howard Orr, Debra Tosch, Robert Macaulay, Tom Andert, Keith Lindley, Denise Corliss, Ann Wichmann, Julie Noyes and their dogs

Lawrence Dubrovich, Joan Pamboukes, Tessa van der Waals, Freek Kuin, Tricia Gabriel, Mike Slack, Anthony Accardi, Tim Groen, Christiane Celle, Stijn Huijts, Lene ter Haar, Galerie Paul Andriesse, Julie Saul, Ulrich Lang and Ron Jude for their support and assistance

DESIGN Tessa van der Waals, Amsterdam
SEPARATIONS AND PRINTING Calff & Meischke, Amsterdam
BINDING Geertsen, Nijmegen

PUBLISHER The Ice Plant, www.theiceplant.cc
DISTRIBUTOR D.A.P./Distributed Art Publishers, www.artbook.com

SECOND PRINTING October 2011

ISBN: 978-0-9823653-6-6